KAIZ_.
and
YOU

Other books by Igor J. Popovich:

Winning at Job Interviews
Your Job – How to Get It, How To Keep It
Managing Consultants

KAIZEN
and
YOU

achieving success through self knowledge
and constant improvement

Igor S. Popovich

2000

First published in Great Britain in 1997 by Management Books 2000 Ltd, Cowcombe House, Cowcombe Hill, Chalford, Gloucestershire GL6 8HP Tel: 01285-760722. Fax: 01285-760708

Printed by Chris Fowler International Ltd, London.

British Library Cataloguing in Publication Data is available

ISBN 1-85252-261-5

Dedication

To individuals who recognise the need for change and improvement; to the new generation of self-developers who are in pursuit of more, better and faster; to the minority who live lives of purpose, not of quiet despair.

Acknowledgements

This book is the result of endless hours of reading, writing, talking to people and living its philosophy. There aren't many new concepts and ideas expressed in this book, although there are some. I cannot take credit for most of them – I have simply combined the most potent and powerful among them and brought them together, organised under a concept which is just being discovered in the West but which is a living philosophy for so many Japanese corporations and individuals: KAIZEN. The concept is plain and simple, but elegant: success through constant and gradual self-actualisation and self-improvement.

KAIZEN and YOU is the treatment of the KAIZEN concept and its applications to individual improvement, as against its applications in the corporate and business environment. Should you wish to learn more about corporate applications of KAIZEN, please consult the excellent book *KAIZEN – the Key to Japan's Competitive Success*, by Masaaki Imai, published by McGraw-Hill, New York.

There are many contributors to this work, yet most of them don't even realise they have contributed. To mention the names would take to much space and could bore you to death. Real evangelists, champions and ambassadors of the good and positive know the value of contribution towards common good. They need no praise or recognition. The bibliography at the end of the book lists some of the priceless works of my teachers and role models. Through reading their books I feel as though I know them personally, which I unfortunately don't. If, after reading this book, you get the same feeling about me, I would feel very honoured indeed.

None of the evangelists to whom I owe a debt of knowledge and enlightenment is responsible for my limited ability to use their contributions in a better or more beneficial way to that used in this work.

Igor S. Popovich
Perth, Australia
January, 1997

Contents

Introduction

Why *KAIZEN and You*?

"The mass of men lead lives of quiet desperation."
David Henry Thoreau

The best way answer this fundamental question is to ask you another one: Who is running your life? It may seem strange to you and you may be inclined to answer automatically: "I am, of course." I challenge you here and now to think about this question. Who is *really* running your life? Is it you or your employer, your Government, your friends and relatives, your children or parents, your spouse or lover, your co-workers or customers, your teachers or students, your neighbours or acquaintances? Maybe it is your fears and phobias, your lack of self-esteem and assertiveness, your lack of knowledge and experience, your poor ethics or poor memory, your ill health or constant debt? Are you *really* running your life?

Well, you may really be running your own life, making your own decisions and living your own dreams, but the chances are that you are not. They say that seventy or more per cent of employees in the Western world are in the wrong job, wishing they could be doing something else and being somewhere else. Two thirds of people on earth do not love their partners or spouses and those marriages end up in divorce; more than one third of adults suffer from some form of depression, either chronic or acute.

It sounds like our fellow human beings have lots of problems on their narrow shoulders. The main culprit is something or somebody else who is running their lives for them. They are not in control, they are not in charge! Even if we free ourselves from all unhealthy and potentially detrimental influences from various sources (politicians, media, employers, friends and relatives, educational and religious systems, and many more) we are very likely to stumble on the last barrier – our own mind, which, paradoxically, in many cases works against us, not for us.

> *"The spirit of self-help is the root of all genuine growth in the individual; and, exhibited in the lives of many, it constitutes the true course of national vigor and strength ..."*

This quote is not from some Japanese or Chinese book on Zen; it's from a best-seller *Self Help*, by one Samuel Smiles, who published it in 1859!

The success of society is based on the success of the individual. The opposite is also true. The success of the individual is much easier to achieve in successful surroundings. Without solving the problems of individuals, the problems of work, corporations, politics and governments cannot possibly be solved, because every problem is in its essence a problem of an individual or groups of individuals.

The Self-Improvement Philosophy

> *"The ideas I stand for are not mine. I borrowed them from Socrates. I swiped them from Chesterfield. I stole them from Jesus. And I put them in a book. If you don't like their rules, whose would you use?"*
> Dale Carnegie

The main theme of *KAIZEN and You* is self-improvement through constant and gradual effort. Results in life are achievable through many means: hard work, cheating, crime, inheritance, luck, use and manipulation of others. Everything we do or don't do produces results, and in most cases are a direct result of our input. This book is about achieving positive, ethical results through constant self-improvement.

Introduction

KAIZEN (pronounced *ky'zen*) is Japanese for a philosophy of constant improvement. It is about success based on one's inner strength which then expands outwards. That one doesn't have to be an individual; it could be a corporation, an institution or a whole society.

Among other principles that will be discussed in this book, *KAIZEN And You* addresses three fundamental questions:

- Is positive mental attitude sufficient for success?
- Is significant improvement possible through the use of traditional, unrelated skills and uncoordinated efforts?
- Are breakthroughs, luck and quantum leaps a solid base for success?

To spare you from anxiety and flipping through the book to find the quick answers, the answer to all three questions is an unequivocal NO. The alternative to these three concepts can be found within these covers.

DEFINITION

KAIZEN in this book means constant and ongoing gradual improvement in every sphere of individual life – personal relationships, spiritual development, career management, intellectual and physical advancement, community betterment, entrepreneurship.

The Purpose Of *KAIZEN and You*

The purpose of *KAIZEN and You* is to provide you with comprehensive, down-to-earth information and advice on how to:

- Get to know yourself better.
- Capitalise on your strengths and neutralise or eliminate your weaknesses.
- Manage people to achieve your goals.
- Speed up your way towards success.
- Become a better, more efficient and resourceful person.

The aim is to define tools you can use for constant improvement and then show you how to use those tools in the best way for your own benefit and for the benefit of others. Should you find other ways to use them, by all means do. As with anything in life, what works for you may not work for me, and vice versa. If you ask me whether the methods outlined in *KAIZEN and You* work all the time, I would have to say that they don't – nothing does. It does, however, work most of the time, and it works well for those who adopt its philosophy or adapt it to suit their circumstances.

STRATEGY

The philosophy, principles and guidelines of KAIZEN should be adopted, but the strategies, tactics and methods described should be analysed, critically evaluated and adapted to suit your own circumstances.

What Kind of Self-improvement Book Is *KAIZEN and You*?

"The proven method of inducing people to buy motivational books is to mix the basics up with a number of psychological words, a sprinkling of anecdotes, a liberal peppering of formulas, spread the mixture between the book covers with lashings of sincerity and

persuasion and serve it up under the guise of a hypnotic 'Get Rich Quick' title."

Ron Holland, *Talk And Grow Rich*

In the light of Ron Holland's very accurate and widely used recipe, *KAIZEN and You* is not a typical self-improvement book. It is *the* self-improvement book, because it won't simply pump you up with the hype of the "believe in yourself" or "the magic of positive thinking" school, like many others in the past, who cloned the same ideas numerous times with worn-out clichés to the point of exhaustion. *KAIZEN and You* is a realistic book. It acknowledges the value of *preparation*, as one of the keys to sustained achievement, and enforces the concept of *consistency* in action, with each self-improvement step leading in the same direction.

DEFINITION

Life is a process of change in which we either progress or regress.

Some brave claims will be found in *KAIZEN and You*. One of them is that a hundred per cent improvement is possible and normal. Initially, that one hundred per cent improvement comes in the form of doing one hundred "little things" one per cent better, instead of trying to do one or a couple of things hundred per cent better. Through the compounding principle of improvement, which illustrates the power of continuous "one per cent" improvement, those bigger jumps in performance are eventually achievable.

Continuous improvement is a process of change, specifically a change for the better, so *KAIZEN and You* is a story about change. The story is laid out as a series of concepts, lessons, ideas and strategies. Although they could be looked at in isolation, the true power of continuous improvement can be achieved only by integrating them into a coherent view and applying that view to your life. The story of KAIZEN has no beginning or end, and the middle is where you want it to be – and that is the very beauty of it: it could be started anytime, applied to any sphere of individual or collective life, in manufacturing, politics, education, writing, relationships. KAIZEN is a common denominator for all of the concepts outlined within these covers, although some of them have a very loose connection with it. It is a theme that serves as a framework, including many other recurring concepts and leitmotifs.

There Are No Case Studies In *KAIZEN and You*

KAIZEN and You is one of the rare non-fiction and management books without case studies. All you'll find here are success stories from real life, involving real people. KAIZEN is already a reality for many people. I hope it will become real for you, too. Many case studies are deceptive and dishonest. It is easy to choose examples and cases that illustrate the author's point of view and the point he wants to make while ignoring instances when the same actions, policies and methods produced completely different results.

Almost half of the corporations singled out as examples of management success by Peters and Waterman in their 1982 work *In Search of Excellence* either don't exist any more or are battling along, trying to stay in business. The management philosophy of that and many other books was to identify companies on the basis of the high results they were achieving and equating those results with their management superiority. It was assumed that their management practices were a direct cause of those outstanding results. So much for the results-oriented approach.

 REFLECTION

The approach of KAIZEN is based on values and commitment. KAIZEN is based on a process-oriented philosophy, instead of outdated results-oriented thinking.

It is the aim of this book to communicate the principles of KAIZEN to readers; it will be left to the readers to relate the concepts to their own lives and frames of reference. *KAIZEN and You* deals primarily with the WHYs of constant improvement, but there are also some HOWs.

In this book there are no jokes either. Jokes are simply stories about predictable situations that have unexpected outcomes. There are no unexpected outcomes in KAIZEN. Your success is planned, lived, analysed and sustained, and the results of that success will be expected.

Why Should You Read *KAIZEN and You*?

"Men are anxious to improve their circumstances, but unwilling to improve themselves; therefore they remain bound."

James Allen

KAIZEN and You is written for people who aim to become victors of circumstances instead of victims of circumstances, for those who refuse to remain the product or sum of outside influences, old, counterproductive habits, random events and luck. If you are one of those who want to be able to make intelligent choices that will empower you and have maximum positive impact on your future, this book is for you. You aim to become a champion.

 EXERCISE

Think about your reasons for accepting the idea of continuous improvement and the key motivators behind your decision to do so.

Why do I want to follow the KAIZEN way?

✍ ....

....

....

....

If you are a champion already, read on anyhow; you may discover something new or something you have not been doing for whatever reason. If you are less than what you can be and you strive for improvement, read this book to equip yourself for the victories ahead of you. If you think you don't need to improve and are happy with the status quo, read the book to get to know the people who will defeat you in the game of life.

Live This Book

This book will challenge you to take control of your life and responsibility for the constant improvement of your professional, communication and interpersonal skills, your integrity, ethics and values. Its aim is to make you a champion in your chosen occupation, in your relationships and in life in general.

I urge you not merely to read this book, but to live it and experience it. By reading it, you will undoubtedly acquire some new information, discover different ways of doing some things you have been doing already and confirm some of your own beliefs, experiences and ways of thinking. This is only the first level of mastery: awareness. You will rise from the bottomless pit of ignorance onto a field of discovery. This will not, however, have a lasting beneficial effect, unless you take the information learned one step further and experience it. Your philosophy of constant improvement has to be a living philosophy. Only a living philosophy can change the way you think, live and behave.

Aikido is a Japanese approach that takes a holistic view of a person. It is about paying attention to various aspects of the whole, but not in isolation from one another. Adopting certain recipes and translating them into clichés will prove useless. Just doing KAIZEN and rendering its teachings into shortcuts will prove equally wrong. You shouldn't just "do" KAIZEN; you have to "think" KAIZEN and be KAIZEN.

EXERCISE

Read this book at least once and then as many times as you need to become comfortable with its ideas and teachings. Then write in the space below your answer to the question, "Shall I choose KAIZEN as my guiding principle and live its philosophy?" The aim of this exercise is for you to become aware of your thoughts provoked by KAIZEN *and* You *and to decide whether the path of continuous improvement is a choice you want to make.*

Shall I choose KAIZEN as my guiding principle in life?

✍ ....

....

....

....

....

....

....

....

....

....

19

1

Embracing Kaizen

And Living Its Philosophy

Why KAIZEN? (The Challenges Ahead)

"Panta rhei." (Everything flows.)
Heraclitus

Constant improvement is a stepping stone to constant growth, and constant growth may be expressed as a pursuit of quantity, quality, innovation and productivity. This applies to both organisations (countries and corporations) and individuals.

Quantity addresses the issue of producing more in the same time and with the same resources. Quality is about doing things better and producing goods and services of superior quality. Innovation is how to do things differently, how to find new markets, products and ideas. Productivity deals with the speed of doing things, with maximising one's investments in the production of valuable goods or services.

KAIZEN is the answer to the challenges ahead.

The challenge of technology and productivity

Despite all the emphasis on change, especially on the rapid pace of technological improvement, it would be a mistake to assume that the future will change considerably; it won't, except in the technological sense. Our past will be mirrored into our future. Basic principles and paradigms that governed the life on Earth have not changed significantly since the early days of civilisation.

It took many years and lots of pride to recognise the importance of a conscious effort to improve productivity, creativity, innovation, to become more customer-oriented, to produce quality products and deliver first-class services. Competition and necessity forced businesses and individuals all over the world to change their ways and mind sets.

DEFINITION

Purpose + Passion + Persistence = Productivity

The challenge of employment

"The future never just happened. It was created."
Will and Ariel Durant, *The Lessons of History*

As the information society spreads across ethnic, religious and economic borders, the globalisation of the world enters its mature stage. The technology brings people who are miles apart together, enables them to relate to each other better and to learn about each other faster than before. Achievements, concerns, new methods and techniques are shared freely for the benefit of all. A wave of change is sweeping societies, and change is always followed by its shadow – fear and concern.

People are becoming increasingly concerned about their future. Their jobs are in danger. The nature of work is changing, old loyalties and promises are gone and forgotten, new flexibility and loose arrangements are becoming the rule, rather than the exception.

Relationships, family values, education, politics and religion all face an uncertain future, which is bound to be different from the past. This is probably the only certainty there is.

DEFINITION

Concern about the future is a starting step towards change.

Many people are becoming increasingly aware that the key to the future may no longer be in our past, but the future itself. The past no longer provides all clues and guidelines for the challenges of the future. The sociological, ecological and technological situations and configurations we are entering have no precedent in the past. The unfamiliar problems of the future will require fresh solutions. Without effective improvement of individual skills and knowledge (and those of the corporations and society as a whole) fresh solutions won't be possible.

REFLECTION

The problems and the challenges of the future require new skills and new, better ways of doing things.

The challenge of society

As individuals living in a society we have an obligation to improve not only ourselves, but also the society we are a part of. We have the right and the duty to become everything we could be by realising our potential. In that process of self-improvement, we have to make a commitment to manage our resources and those that belong to society, responsibly and properly. This is the challenge of the individual.

By committing our time, energy, knowledge, financial and other resources to our own advancement, we also contribute towards the common good. We create our own foundations for the future. Every action we take has a definite impact on our future and that of others, no matter how small or insignificant that action may seem. Those individual impacts interact and create synergetic effects that affect our reality in many significant ways. This is why our lives and actions cannot be separated from the needs of society.

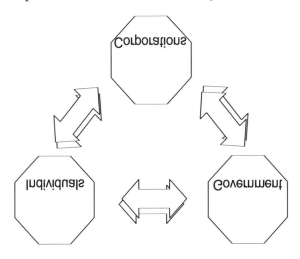

Figure 1. KAIZEN links.

The development of the individual and society as a whole did not, unfortunately, follow the qualitative and quantitative developments of our technology. New, pressing problems and issues are becoming less and less problems of technology and more and more people's problems. Although the push for improvement is now focused on the improvement of "software" or the human factor, there isn't enough conscious, creative effort directed towards the systematic improvement of the individual compared with the widespread drive for better products and services.

The challenge of government

The prevailing disappointment with the way we are governed and the lack of trust in politicians is based primarily on the view that governments serve their own self-justifying purposes instead of serving the interests of individuals, corporations and society as a whole. The under-led and over-governed society sees governments as detached from ordinary people and uncooperative to the business sector.

The room for improvement in the links between governments and their individual and corporate subjects is vast and the progress is not only possible, but desperately needed. The issue lends itself well to kaizen-style gradual improvement and could be a most demanding application of KAIZEN philosophy in the years to come.

KAIZEN Is About Mastery

Achieving mastery in any area of human endeavour, any craft or vocation or any sphere of private or business life requires two basic ingredients – time and effort. This is especially so in the early stages, in the delicate, tender, demanding beginnings. Self-improvement is no different. In the beginning, it requires an enormous effort, unconditional commitment and long hours, yet the results achieved are only symbolic. Then, slowly but surely, the same actions and efforts start producing greater, more significant results. The orchard you are tending starts to bear more and more fruit.

Many processes in life exhibit the same law. If the dependency between achievement and effort is plotted on a graph, it would resemble a stretched letter S. That is why the curve was named the "S-curve" (Figure 2).

Mastery is one of the key concepts of this book. Mastery is a way of living, a vehicle for advancement through constant and gradual improvements, restructuring yourself, redefining your mission, goals and priorities, enhancing and compounding your skills and knowledge and integrating them into a coherent and consistent philosophy. This philosophy has to become your living philosophy.

Mastery cannot be improvised or faked. It has to be achieved through deliberate effort and conscious choices which will help you to cease being a product of chance, luck, random decisions and external influences. Mastery takes time, as long as you want it and allow it to take.

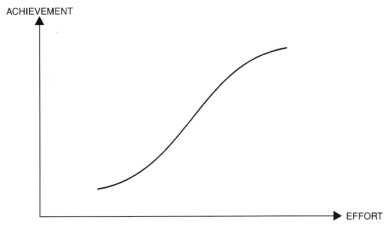

Figure 2. The "S-curve".

REFLECTION

KAIZEN is not a linear process! Nothing in the world is linear; there is no straight lines in nature, just curves.

KAIZEN Is Never Growing Up

"The way a child discovers the world constantly replicates the way science began. You start to notice what's around you, and you get very curious about how things work. How things interrelate. It's as simple as seeing a bug that intrigues you. You want to know where it goes at night; who its friends are; what it eats."

David Cronenberg, *Cronenberg On Cronenberg*

"What are you going to be when you grow up?" When I was a kid, this was one of our favourite questions, the one we used to initiate endless talks and dreams about our future, the things we wanted to achieve, places we wanted to travel to and the people we wanted to become like. Growing up was seen as a magical, mysterious and challenging process, in which we were about to become strong, just, good-hearted, loved, respected and, generally, happy.

Although we didn't know how the actual process of maturing and growing up worked, and although most of us were happy just being kids, we somehow desired that growing up started as soon as possible, so we can immediately be all those things, and more. We hardly realised that growing up is a continuous process and the very essence of life – not a time-bound sequence of steps that are taken to arrive at a destination and then live happily ever after. Picture books portrayed that sort of philosophy and painted a picture of a princess who, saved from some sort of danger by a handsome prince, married him and "they lived happily ever after". The question that started to puzzle me at some stage is what really happened "ever after"? What did the Prince and his princess do, how did they fill their days and how did their life story develop from that point on?

To find the answer to that question I had to wait almost thirty years. It became obvious that either the picture books blatantly lied to us or something was wrong with the "real life" and its protagonists, the children I grew up with and others who entered the mature age. We didn't fit the stereotypes portrayed in books and adventure stories. Not many of us became explorers, heroes, scientists, travellers, writers, leaders or the great athletes we read about and dreamt about being like. We became storemen, housewives, mechanics, sales assistants, filling clerks. Some were long-term unemployed, many married early and divorced soon after, others were drowning their sorrows in alcohol or tried to escape the realities and return to the old dream world through drugs. Many stopped growing up and started growing old, and growing old was not among the dreams and hopes they had.

"What are you going to be when you grow up?" is the wrong question, simply because the winners in life never grow up – they keep growing. I don't want to grow up any more. I want to stay young in heart, with open mind and zest for life, new challenges and achievements. I can only hope you are the same, and have a good reason to believe you are. The very fact that you started reading this book is an achievement in itself. Did you know that only about five per cent of people in a developed country such as the United States, Australia or the United Kingdom will buy or read a book this year? Without knowing it, you have already made the top five per cent! The sad fact (supported by research) is that only about ten per cent of people who start reading a book actually finish it. I can only hope that you'll be among them.

Never growing up is the one of the fundamental themes of this book. It is also one of the traits of the "champions" in the game of life. Throughout our journey together, I will refer to this term for lack of a more appropriate one. Labelling people as winners or losers is a very dangerous practice. Every one of us wins some battles and loses some (even the champions). We all make errors and miss out on opportunities.

However, the definition of a "champion" that will be an underlying motif through the pages that follow is based on certain premises. Champions are not paralysed by their past routines. They are not afraid of change, which means constantly analysing themselves, planning their course of action, setting goals and monitoring their progress towards those goals. It also means they are prepared to embark on a course of constant self-improvement through consistent and concentrated effort and through maintaining control despite uncertainty, ambiguity and adversity. This constant self-improvement is the main theme of this book.

 STORY

Hans Beck is a toy-maker with Playmobil. "I wanted to make a toy that could force the children to use their fantasy. Kids get bored with toys that 'do something'. They use them three times, then run out of stories, and put them aside."

Horst Brandstatter, the company leader, complements Beck: "The idea is not that the toy has to do something, but that the children do something with the toy. The children like simple things. They have ideas you and I cannot see."

KAIZEN Is About Quality

When quality is mentioned, we usually associate it with the quality of products and services. This kind of quality is a major concern of managers, production lines and Total Quality Management gurus. Quality, as defined in this book, is also the quality of the individual – you. KAIZEN for the individual could be described as the process of becoming better, more productive and a more successful member of society, therefore contributing more towards common good.

 FURTHER READING: *Quality is Free*

Phillip Crosby's book is by far the best and the most readable book on quality. Although he talks about managing quality in corporations and instituting quality control systems in organisations, many points and rules apply to individuals and groups who strive to make their lives better and more successful. Crosby describes his work as "The art of making quality certain". The most memorable feature of his book is the last chapter titled "Guidelines for Browsers", where all the main points are summarised, like a book of psalms for quality believers. If you don't read the book, read those guidelines at least.(Crosby, P.B., Mentor, New York, 1980)

KAIZEN Is A Religion

"My religion consists of a humble admiration of the illimitable superior spirit who reveals himself in the slight details we are able to perceive with our frail and feeble mind."
                                                                Albert Einstein

In Japan, KAIZEN is a religion, bigger than Buddhism, Shintoism or Catholicism, simply because it has more followers than any of those teachings. It is not a mere tool any more, but a whole way of living life and doing business. Akio Morita, chairman of Sony Corporation, links various religious influences with the outlook towards constant improvement:

> *"We Japanese do not think of ourselves as deeply religious people, although we are; we tend to believe that God resides in everything. We are Buddhists, Confucians, Shintoists, and Christians, but we are also very pragmatic. We often joke that most Japanese are born Shinto, live a Confucian life, get married Christian-style, and have a Buddhist funeral. We have our rites and customs and festivals steeped in centuries of religious tradition, but we are not bound by taboos and feel free to try everything and seek the best and most practical ways of doing things."[2]*

ACTION

Become an evangelist for the KAIZEN cause.Practise what you preach and preach what you practise.

KAIZEN Is A Quest

KAIZEN is a never ending quest for improvement, a race without a finishing line. As a quest, KAIZEN is concerned with your growth and with finding purpose in doing the right things and doing them right. It is a quest that starts with the realisation that you are not all you could be and that you could be more than you ever dreamt you could be.

The aim of KAIZEN is to keep succeeding on your own terms, always on a slightly higher level than before, to make the best of your abilities and opportunities. Absolute best is not the aim; it is your personal best, the best possible at a particular time, in a particular place and in the particular circumstances. KAIZEN recognises that the ultimate level is never reached: the finishing line in such a quest always recedes and is always ahead. Self-improvement is a lifetime pursuit.

In the Western culture, one's progression through life is typically evaluated in terms of advancements in a chosen career, levels of achievements and personal material wealth accumulated. Oriental cultures evaluate one's journey through life from the aspect of improvement one's inner nature or being. In Japan, this concept is called *kokoro*. *Kokoro* is based on the notion that merely doing and achieving is a meaningless, empty pursuit unless it also results in enlightenment, wisdom and betterment of one's mind, character and soul. *Kokoro* says that it is not only the end destination that matters, but the journey towards that destination (the real meaning of our efforts) should make us better, deeper and wiser.

DEFINITION

KAIZEN is about seeking solutions that work, inventing the tools that produce results, delivering promises we make, standing for what makes sense, setting our goals and moving towards them, engineering a future that makes sense to us.

KAIZEN Is Pragmatic And Humanistic

KAIZEN is a pragmatic approach. Pragmatic means that its basis is experience and real life results, rather than theory and hypotheses. Practical actions that produce practical results and provide practical experience are the foundations of the self-improvement philosophy. The approach is pragmatic, its views are practical, no-nonsense, without hype or emotional expenditure.

Throughout your self-improvement development, judging ideas and concepts by their practical consequences and appropriateness to your own situation and preferences is fundamentally a pragmatic approach. Improvement methods have to be adapted to your own context, not blindly adopted and followed without critical evaluation. Methods that work for others and in a different context may not work for you.

The opposite also applies. You may find out that some ideas and methods that work well for you do not produce the same results when practised by others. This is perfectly normal. With this in mind, one can say that KAIZEN is also individualistic in its details and various applications, although the concept itself and its basic postulates and overall philosophy are certainly communal in nature and pluralist in structure (it contains a multitude of concepts).

In this book, KAIZEN is also a humanistic approach. Humanistic means that it's centred on the individual and that it believes that every individual has the power to change and improve for his or her own good and for the benefit of the family, employers and society as a whole.

In terms of the relationship between various activities, interdependence and relationships between various spheres of individual and collective life, KAIZEN is a pantheistic philosophy. Natural and human activities are seen as a whole, and that holistic view of life integrates various aspects into a coherent total, be it the life of an individual, a corporation or a whole society.

DEFINITION

KAIZEN ensures that:

- *opportunities are not missed, but recognised and acted upon;*

- *problems are solved by removing the sources of problems;*

- *optimal alternatives are chosen and right choices are made;*

- *change is embraced and welcomed;*

- *change results in improvement, not in a change for change's sake;*

- *achieved improved become permanent through maintenance.*

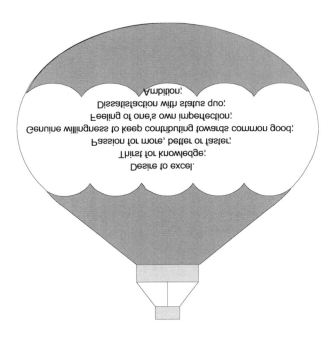

Ambition.
Dissatisfaction with status quo.
Feeling of one's own imperfection.
Genuine willingness to keep contributing towards common good.
Passion for more, better or faster.
Thirst for knowledge.
Desire to excel.

Figure 3. The KAIZEN balloon – things that lead to KAIZEN.

Status Quo And Quantum Leaps

The KAIZEN philosophy assumes that the fundamentals of what is to be improved are right; it does NOT search for breakthroughs and quantum leaps, through innovation, drastic improvements or lucky breaks. Those radical changes occur frequently, often helped by constant improvement. Many new ideas, discoveries and innovative, creative concepts and products sprang into life during efforts to improve older, inferior products, concepts or methods. KAIZEN assumes that your way of life and your psyche deserve continuous improvement. It is not a one-off occurrence, a "once-in-a-blue-moon" phenomenon. It's not dramatic or immediately visible either, but subtle and profound.

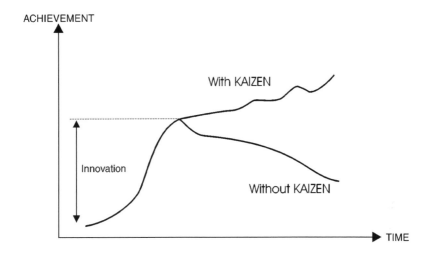

Figure 4. How KAIZEN relates to innovation.

KAIZEN Is A Generic Term

"Take the understanding of the East and the knowledge of the West – and then seek."

Gurdjieff

The principles and the philosophy of KAIZEN can be applied in every sphere of life and to every aspect of living. Its teachings are equally beneficial to individuals and corporations, to employers and employees, to parents and children. The teachings are the same; only the applications change. The more applications you find for KAIZEN in your private, intimate, professional and social life, the better you integrate improvements achieved in various aspects of your life and the better you apply winning strategies from one area to others, the more KAIZEN will do for you.

DEFINITION

KAIZEN is a generic term and can be successfully applied to many aspects of both individual and corporate activities.

Continuous improvement is one way of avoiding the false starts and dead ends which are associated with uncoordinated efforts, quick fixes and short-term solutions. KAIZEN is a strategic framework which helps to organise and synthesise achievements, resources and actions into a coherent, systematic pattern of improvement.

STORY

One day a famous Japanese business executive paid a visit to a well-known Zen master to discuss Zen's relevance to management. Following Japanese etiquette, the master served green tea. When the visitor's cup was full, the master kept pouring; the tea overflowed.

The executive was startled. "The cup is full; no more will go in." Said the master, "Like this cup, you are full of your own thoughts. How can I show you Zen unless you first empty your cup?"[3]

KAIZEN Can Be Started Anytime, But The Best Time Is Now!

"The beginning is the most important part of the work."
Plato

When is the best time to start your self-improvement programme? Compared to never starting at all, any time is the right time to start. The best time is now! No matter what your situation in life is and what steps, big or small, you are presently taking towards fulfilling your dreams and becoming what you want to become, small, steady betterment won't take much of your time or effort. Incremental improvements can be undertaken any time, anywhere, anyhow, even if bigger, more significant changes are in the making.

KAIZEN is based on what is, not on what was or what could or ought to be. Improvement starts with what is, what you are and what you have and is directed towards what you could be and could have. The beneficial results of KAIZEN when compounded and constantly refined will last over time and even grow steadily as long as continuous improvement is practised.

KAIZEN Requires Good Memory

"You have to begin to lose your memory, if only in bits and pieces, to realize that memory is what makes our lives. Life without memory is no life at all, just as an intelligence without the possibility of expression is not really an intelligence. Our memory is our coherence, our reason, our feeling, even our action. Without it, we are nothing."

Luis Buñuel, *My Last Sigh*

To learn from the past events and actions, to follow trends and recognise patterns, to remember which solutions worked and which didn't and to ascertain what types of problems required what types of solutions are some of the aims of capitalising on your memory.

"What we call learning is only a process of recollection," said Socrates. The same statement can be applied to KAIZEN. Improvement is not something that originates outside an individual, something foreign to him, something imposed or enforced upon him. Improvement is a natural progression in life, a natural state or condition. Discovering new ways of doing things and doing them better, faster, cheaper and with more satisfaction is improvement. All those desires for improvement are already present in every one of us, so KAIZEN is only a quest for eliciting something that already exists, no matter how implicitly, latently or well hidden or suppressed it may be.

Accurate records serve the same purpose. In a rapidly changing environment, where communications are fast and information needs to be accessed quickly, your memory may not be accurate enough to rely upon. An effective method of recording various facts and figures, ideas and thoughts is your insurance policy against time and forgetfulness.

Wherever you go, whatever you do, always carry a notebook and a pen or use a miniature tape recorder. Inspiration, enlightenment and ideas may come at any time, any place. Act on them promptly by jotting down as much information as the situation permits.

The ultimate aim, however, is not knowledge about the past, but the application of that knowledge to your present and future endeavours. Adapting your experience to various situations that lie in front of you is the quest of KAIZEN.

KAIZEN Takes Time

"If we try to go quick, quick, we end up going slow, slow."
Old Tibetan saying

KAIZEN is not about success overnight. Most personal, family or organisational improvements take time to achieve and the self-improvement climate takes time to cultivate. Sustaining continuous incremental improvements over a prolonged period requires patience and perseverance.

To recognise the validity of the continuous improvement idea and to agree with it takes only an instant. The understanding of its principles and teachings can be achieved in a relatively short time. Nevertheless, neither is sufficient for the achievement of worthwhile practical results. For that, an intimate knowledge and awareness of the principles behind the process is required, which can only take place in its own time and at its own pace. The awareness and the new quality of life KAIZEN aims for spring from a commitment to the process and from remaining true to it despite not knowing how long it will take to achieve the desired results.

STORY

Wallace Rasmussen's first job in Beatrice Foods Co. was to hoist ice blocks in the dairy plant. His natural aptitude for mechanics and electrical engineering eventually helped him to become a crane operator, maintenance man and chief engineer.

He then became plant manager, district manager, regional vice-president, senior vice-president and the chief executive officer of the largest food-processing company in America. When ask to designate a turning point in his career, he answered:

"No, there hasn't been one as far as I am concerned because every day that went by I was better off than the day before. As long as I can remember my main objective was that tomorrow I wanted to be just a little better than I was today. And I always say, just take it one step at a time."[14]

What Kind Of Improvements Can KAIZEN Bring?

In a book such as this it isn't easy to produce specific examples of improvements that would be of interest to most readers. Each one of us has his or her own problems, cares about different things and strives towards different goals in life. To illustrate the philosophy of continuous improvement in various areas of our lives, here is a list of a few common statements that describe a situation or a problem which can be successfully resolved through the use of KAIZEN techniques.

Since gradual improvement encompasses many steps and phases of development, it isn't possible to list all of the detailed ones here. Please accept some generalisation for the sake of clarity and comprehension of this exercise.

You will notice that the first step in the improvement journey has already been made in the examples below. The problem is stated in simple and clear terms. In many specific issues you may face in your life, those problems will not be formulated for you; you will have to do that yourself. Recognising things for what they are is often a difficult aspect of the improvement game.

The steps you could choose to follow in devising your improvement plan could be:

- State the problem.
- Consider contributing factors.
- Explore options.
- Select one or more options to be implemented.
- Put those options into practice.
- Monitor progress and take corrective actions.
- Keep moving towards the successful resolution of the issue.

Alternatively, if you prefer, devise your own sequence of actions and apply it to your reality. The main point you should remember is that improvements can be made in all spheres of life. No matter what your problem is, continuous improvement can and will help you in finding the solution.

The statements below are selected from various aspects of life. Some of them may be relevant to you, others may be applicable to someone else. All of them can be successfully resolved through continuous improvement.

- I am overweight, in poor shape, obese.
- I am not good at mathematics.
- My spelling is terrible.
- My vocabulary is limited.
- I am afraid of speaking in public.
- My husband complains about my cooking.
- I always spend more than I earn and cannot get out of my debts.
- My memory is poor.
- At work, nobody appreciates my efforts and achievements.
- I am terrified of computers, but have to learn to use them on my job.

- I don't have enough time to do things I want or have to do.
- We like our beautiful house, but it's becoming rather small for our growing family.
- I don't have many friends and don't know how to expand my circle of friends.
- My wife complains about my long hours at work and our relationship suffers.

Does KAIZEN Always Work?

"Don't be afraid to take a big step if one is indicated. You can't cross a chasm in two small jumps."

David Lloyd George

No, KAIZEN doesn't always work – nothing does. Continuous gradual improvement is exactly that – a continuous effort to achieve more, better and faster in small, gradual steps. In many life situations a different approach is needed – one has to break with the past, change a direction completely and start afresh. In such a case there would be no point in constant improvement if it leads in the wrong direction.

Constant improvement also doesn't include (or exclude) innovation, quantum leaps and breakthroughs. Those significant discoveries of things new, different or something unrelated that becomes related (or vice versa), become a starting point for new levels of constant improvements, which then start from a different plateau and assume new directions.

Some of you reading these lines may think that KAIZEN won't work for you. Others may have been asking themselves: what if KAIZEN works? What if it brings changes to my life, makes me different, alters my relationships, my career, the games I have been playing? You may be afraid of change, of the unknown, unexplored, inexperienced. If you are, you have to admit it to yourself, and you have to realise that gradual improvement leads to gradual change, possibly the least difficult and the least traumatic way of dealing with change.

FURTHER READING:

KAIZEN – The Key To Japanese Competitive Success

Masaaki Imai introduced the world of KAIZEN to Western managers through this classic. This handbook on corporate application of KAIZEN shows 16 KAIZEN management practices and their application in total quality control programmes, just-in-time production, problem-solving, maintenance, customer satisfaction, profit planning and other important aspects of corporate life.(Imai, M., Random House, New York, 1986)

2

Adopting The KAIZEN Qualities

Steady Pace

"By the time it came to the edge of the Forest the stream had grown up, so that it was almost a river, and, being grown-up, it did not run and jump and sparkle along as it used to do when it was younger, but moved more slowly. For it knew now where it was going, and it said to itself, 'There is no hurry. We shall get there some day.'"

A. A. Milne

Western culture is based on the philosophy that says if a method or a plan doesn't produce fast results, something has to be changed immediately. KAIZEN teaches that successful strategies and tactics cannot simply be turned on and off at the first sign of problem or adversity. Staying power, sticking to the plan and persistence are the key concepts of a successful improvement plan.

The most common reason for individual, entrepreneurial and corporate failure today is the school of thought that makes people think things are going to happen overnight. Everything takes time and a steady pace is the optimal progression towards success. Quantum leaps and significant breakthroughs are just an exception that confirms the rule.

Steady pace of the continuous, incremental changes and improvements involves less risk than a self-improvement strategy based on one or a few major changes, which require a considerable investment of time, money, energy and other resources. In terms of effectiveness, incremental improvements can add up to a level normally achieved by those "breakthrough" improvements.

QUESTION

You have to climb to the top of a mountain. Would you move briskly, through a series of fast climbs, followed by a rest period or would you move steadily, at a slow pace, but without stopping?

Awareness

"A human action becomes genuinely important when it springs from the soil of a clear-sighted awareness of the temporality and the ephemerality of everything human. It is only this awareness that can breathe any greatness into an action."

Vaclav Havel

From the awareness point of view, there are three groups of people:

- Those who don't know they got a problem and don't know what to do about it. They are ignorant.

- Those who know they've got a problem, but don't know what to do about it. Even if they do know what could be done, they never act in order to resolve the issues. They are aware.

- Those who know they've got a problem, and know what to do about it, but also take appropriate actions towards solving them. They are the self-improvers.

DEFINITION

Awareness + Risk-taking = Growth

Achievement is the inevitable and natural product of awareness. Increase your awareness level. Examine your senses. Analyse your feelings. Step out of various routines and search for other, different ways of doing things. Consider doing things you haven't currently been doing or haven't done before. Feel the world around you. Pay attention to sounds, smells, colours, textures, shapes. Look for the unusual, strange, mysterious, unexplainable, but don't neglect the ordinary and simple. Notice others. Pay attention to what they do, what they say, how they act; then ask yourself why are they acting or feeling that way. Observe how they react to you and to each other. In two simple words: be alive!

REFLECTION

Status quo is a myth. You are either improving and getting in front, or getting worse and lagging behind.

Action

"It is easier to earn a living by doing something others are not doing."

Akio Morita, Chairman of Sony

In my school days I liked soccer and I dreamt about becoming a famous goalkeeper. I enjoyed playing for my school's team and spending hours trying to prevent players from scoring. At some stage I realised that I was more inclined towards intellectual pursuits and that I wasn't prepared to sacrifice everything and spend endless hours sweating and training hard.

I shall always remember what my coach once said to me: "When you see a high ball entering the penalty area, you have two basic choices – to stay on the line and position yourself in the best possible spot or to leave the line at the right moment and run towards it so you can grab it before the opponent gets hold of it. If you leave the line, you have to do it right, you have to go all the way. If you are going to go only halfway, you shouldn't even bother to do it. You will not get the ball and at the same time you will leave your goal unprotected and create a dangerous empty space behind you."

For some reason I remembered that simple advice well. Later in life I realised how important it was. It summarised quite well the basic requirements for taking actions in life:

- Realise that action has to be taken. This is the question of awareness – the appreciation that something has to be done.

- Decide when is the right time to take the action. This is the question of timing – the sense of when to do certain things.

- Analyse your options and, based on the available information, select one course of action. This is the question of choice.

- Once you are in action, wholeheartedly go all the way; don't stop until you carry out what you set to do. This is the question of implementation and persistence – how well you carry it out and how courageous and persistent you are to carry it through.

DEFINITION

Four pillars of action: awareness, timing, choice, persistence.

Learn from your actions. Let that learning become the basis for your future actions; let those reflections and introspection become a habit. Learning from actions is a trial-and-error, heuristic process of gradual change, which requires commitment to learning and which often means making mistakes in finding out what are the right things to do and what are the best ways of doing them. This incremental action-learning-action-learning process is the very core of all self-improvement philosophy. It is the *sine qua non* of success.

REFLECTION

Old, worn-out actions produce old, worn-out results.New, fresh actions produce new, fresh results.

Making Right Choices

"If to do were as easy as to know what were good to do, chapels had been churches and poor men's cottages princes' palaces."
William Shakespeare

Making right choices and doing things right the first time are now well accepted concepts of W. Edwards Deming's quality control philosophy. It is also an important building block of KAIZEN philosophy. Time is precious; it is the only limited or scarce commodity in the life of an individual. Doing things again and again costs time and money and deprives you of the lost opportunity.

Before you make a decision or a choice of importance, you first have to conclude and appreciate the fact that a choice or decision has to be made; that you can't simply ignore the issue and hope it will go away. The next step is to recognise various demands that have to be met for you to succeed. Those demands and the assessment of potential risks attached to various options will have an impact on the final decision you make. This is a typical decision-making pattern. Follow it and watch your decision-making skills and habits improve significantly.

PARADOX

People act and make choices on emotion, and then try to justify those actions and choices and back them up with reason.

Balance

"I balanced all, brought all to mind,
The years to come seemed waste of breath,
A waste of breath the years behind,
In balance with this life, this death."

W. B. Yeats

Balance could simply be described as a feeling of orientation amidst options determined by the relationship of restraining and progressive forces. Balance gives us a sense where we are in any given situation, preventing us from becoming entangled in details while dealing with pressures of the moment and empowering us by not losing the sight of our priorities and ultimate aims.

Balance is a relationship between giving and receiving, between the concern for your own well-being and the concern for others, between doing things you have to do and those you like doing. In a self-improvement sense, you should strive for a balance between your various roles. There will always be some areas of your life that will demand more attention and effort, but such investments of time, energy and other resources in certain areas should not be made at the expense of other, equally important ones.

During our lives we play various roles. The same person behaves differently in various environments, at various times and in the company of different people. In one day he may be a son, a father, a husband, a friend, a neighbour, a boss, a subordinate, a customer, a member of his profession, and play many other roles. In some of them he will perform well and feel comfortable with. In others, he will be less successful, while maybe even failing miserably in a few of them.

Ultimately, it is not possible to sustain success and do right in one area in life while doing wrong or failing in others. The balanced nature of life as an invisible whole would be endangered and a cause-effect relationship between different aspects of life would lead to ultimate failure in all areas and departments. Similarly, compartmentalisation of corporations, where some departments are considered to be "profit generators" while others are "making a loss", makes it very difficult, if not outright impossible, to sustain success on a global and long-term level.

"Consequently, the appetitive element of a self-controlled man must be in harmony with the guidance of reason. For the aim of both his appetite and his reason is to what is noble. The appetite of a self-controlled man is directed at the right objects, in the right way, and at the right time; and this is what the reason prescribes."[5] KAIZEN is precisely about a balanced, reasonable approach to different areas of our lives.

EXERCISE

Consider various roles you play in your life. Think about them and analyse them. Which ones do you feel comfortable with? What are the reasons for not feeling so comfortable with the others?

The roles I like playing:

✍ ....

....

....

The roles I don't like playing:

✍ ....

....

....

Passion

"What is passion? It is surely the becoming of a person. Are we not, for most of our lives, marking time? Most of our being is at rest, unlived. In passion, the body and the spirit seek expression outside of self. Passion is all that is other from self."

John Boorman, British film maker

Make your passion your career. If you don't enjoy your job, find another you will enjoy. Get out before it's too late. Up to eighty per cent of people in USA, UK and Australia are misemployed – they are in the wrong jobs! Working only for money and losing your spirit and dignity is a very high price to pay for unhappiness.

Most people, including you and me, have more than one talent. They have a potential that could be developed in several fields and occupations. A path to fulfilment and self-actualisation is to select and develop a talent we feel passionate about and concentrate our efforts not only on doing the right things, but on doing those right things right, the way they should be done. A sure path to misery is being stuck in a job and daily routine we detest and feel bad about.

It shouldn't be hard to realise what your passion is. Your dream is your passion. It is the idea that follows you wherever you go and whatever you do; it is the cause you think or talk about, an obsession that never leaves you, that grows stronger with time and becomes clearer as it grows with you.

EXERCISE

Think about the sources of passion in your life. What do you feel strongly about? What issues are important to you?

Things, people, places, ideas and concepts I feel passionate about:

✐ ....

....

....

Tending The Roots

Directly translated from Japanese, *nemiwashi* means tending to the roots. It sums up a few very important concepts that can be applied to KAIZEN, such as going back to basics, getting the fundamentals right, and building success strategies on a firm, solid and sound base.

STORY

Chinese bamboo is a fascinating plant. It's a plant with a purpose. Its mission is to teach us, humans, the value of constant care, patience and persistence towards our goals. Look what happens when you plant the seeds: you water them and fertilise a bit. But for the first year nothing happens. You decide to continue watering and fertilising for another year, but again, nothing happens. You keep doing your bit for a couple of years more, but there is still no sight of a plant. And then, during your fifth year of tender loving care, something wonderful takes place: in a mere six weeks, the bamboo grows to a remarkable height of more than 25 metres.

*The question is: did the bamboo grow 25 metres in six weeks or in five years? The answer is in five years. By tending the roots, you nurtured the plant. Without such constant loving care it would surely die. This is the best illustration for **nemiwashi**.*

Think of KAIZEN and your self-improvement philosophy as a garden which you nourish and expand over time. You tend to the roots, you fertilise and water it regularly, take the weeds out, fight bugs and diseases. You also plan your garden, you choose a layout that will maximise the resources at your disposal: the size of the garden, its shape, the characteristics of the soil, the number of sunshine hours. The seeds and plants you grow are carefully chosen to maximise the good points of your garden and the climate and to minimise the not so favourable ones. You plant trees, shrubs and flowers that look good together and live in harmony with each other. That symbiotic synergy of your garden will make it stronger and healthier.

The power of expectation works both in your garden and in life. If you plant a birch tree, this is exactly what you are going to get in a couple of years – a beautiful, tender birch tree. There is no way that seedling could turn into a pine tree or a chestnut tree. Seeds never grow some other kind of plant except their own.

Ideas, dreams and expectations behave in a similar way to the seeds you use in your garden. The seed of every achievement and success is first planted in your mind. Over time, that seed will grow and bear fruit. If your mind plants a seed of success, the fruit you are going to reap will be the sweet fruit of success. If, on the other hand, your mind is full of negative thoughts, worries and self-defeating attitudes, the fruit you'll end up with will be the sour fruit of failure.

This is a brief description of the power of expectation. Whatever your mind expects, it will eventually get. If you expect success, it isn't likely that you'll fail. If you expect failure, success is almost impossible.

FURTHER READING: The Little Prince

The Little Prince cannot be found among adult fiction. This is a children's book with a profound message to adults. The little prince travels from planet to planet, all of a miniature size and inhabited by only one person. He talks to a king who has no subjects, a businessman who "owns" the stars, a conceited man who needs someone to admire him, a tippler who drinks to forget that he is ashamed of drinking, a lamplighter who lights a lamp every minute, a geographer who knows nothing about his planet. They all search for or deal with the "matters of consequence", while the little prince watches sunsets, looks for a friendship and cares about his rose. He finally meets a fox, who teaches him a simple, but important secret, that one can see rightly only through the heart, because what is essential is invisible to the eye. There are many important messages and simple secrets of responsibility, care and happiness. Send a copy of this book to all your friends and enemies. (Antoine de Saint-Exupery, William Heinemann Ltd, London, 1986)

Simplification

"People admire complexity. They don't trust something that looks too simple. But only the simple ideas will work. The more powerful ideas have an elegant simplicity about them. Less is more."
Al Ries and Jack Trout, in *Horse Sense (The key to success is finding a horse to ride)*

As humans, with a social nature on the one hand and a need for solitude on the other, probably due to our extraordinary ability to think, reason and evaluate, we overvalue complexity and undervalue simplicity. Despite the power of elegant simplicity, which can be seen and recognised in many ideas, methods and products, there is an ever present human attachment to complexity. The simple is seldom trusted, while the complex is often glorified.

Our world is too complex and too unpredictable to be dealt with without simplification. The number of variables and problems we are able to deal with simultaneously is limited. Most schemes and systems in society are constructed around a finite, limited number of variables. That number is usually two: we talk about left and right, up and down, right and wrong, good and evil, the Government and the Opposition, husbands and wives, workers and employers. Duality seems to be our preference. More than two is a mess.

The main problem with simplification is to know which parts, aspects or descriptors of a problem or issue should be taken into account and which ones should be disregarded in dealing with that issue or problem. This isn't, however, the only danger of simplification. To understand a situation, an issue or a problem, we analyse it by breaking it down into components and by looking each in turn. Quite often, the sense of the whole is lost in that process, because the interactions, dependencies and synergy between those components are ignored.

Simplification in continuous improvement is therefore a necessity, although both a desirable practice and a problem. Simple solutions are often the best, but to arrive at those solutions we have to study and understand complex forces that shape the world. Simple actions taken regularly are better than complex interventions taken when it's too late. Simplification is both a friend and a foe to KAIZEN, just as fire is a good servant, but poor master.

EXERCISE

Consider various aspects of your life and different issues, relationships or problems that make it more complicated than it could be. Then decide on the practical steps you will take to simplify them.

This is how I will simplify my life:

✍..

....

....

In any self-improvement process, the obstacles, confusing issues, the useless, the imagined, the overrated and the decorative should be discarded, put aside or realistically analysed in order to reveal the real issues, the genuine problems and inadequacies. Reducing issues down to their lowest common denominators is simplification. Simple solutions are elegant solutions, and simple solutions work best. But to have the courage to try simple solutions and the confidence in the positive outcomes of those solutions, you have to perceive your problems as simple issues. Your impression of your own inadequacies will determine what kinds of solutions you are going to come up with and what success will those solutions have.

Cutting down through the layers of complexity is like peeling an onion. The useless layers close to the surface are removed in order to arrive at the valuable core. Simplicity and miniaturisation are two typically Japanese concepts. Both are evident in many aspects of oriental life, such as Zen philosophy, minimalist *haiku* poetry and the functional simplicity and user-friendliness of Japanese designs.

Simple ideas and concepts are superior to the complex ones. Simplicity is elegance, efficiency, effectiveness, stewardship and innovation combined and elevated to a level where there is nothing unnecessary, odd, out of place, unwanted or redundant. Instead of coping with complexity concentrate on eliminating it.

 STORY

The game of charades has been around for a long time. Rob Angel's idea was to make a product out of it. He devised formal rules, added a board and included a box with word cards. Angel changed the name to Pictionary. The rest, as they say, is not only history, but also a very illustrative example of success achieved through improving a simple, but sound product, rather than inventing a new and complex one.

Long-Term Vision

"The real voyage of discovery consists not in seeking new lands, but in seeing with new eyes."

Marcel Proust

The most common reason for frustration, low self-esteem, jealousy and failure is short-term thinking. Short-term frame of mind, instant gratification, fast buck, quick fix and quick results have to be replaced with long-term vision. Long-term vision is a product of a strategic self-improvement culture, which is founded on our values, standards, beliefs, goals, behaviour patterns and thinking paradigms. It is framed by the ways we think, what we think about, what we do and how we get things done.

Building a self-improvement culture within yourself also builds your long-term vision. Future opportunities and possibilities open in a succession as you keep focusing on change and implementing positive, coherent and focused actions that determine your strategic behaviour.

STRATEGY

The success of KAIZEN is based on delaying or fore-going instant gratification for the sake of long-term benefits.

The ability and commitment to delay gratification and to undertake bigger, long-term projects is based on the willingness to postpone reaping the rewards of one's actions and compounding those rewards to achieve higher payoffs in the longer term. Many project their happiness into some future time, close or distant, believing that their present situation is just a temporary, passing stage, which will be followed by a more meaningful and prosperous part of their lives. This attitude of hope, without positive actions, no matter how significant they may be, is not what continuous improvement is about. Going back to our analogy with a garden or an orchard, the self-improvement steps taken may span many months or even years:

- Decide which seeds you are going to sow and select them carefully.
- Prepare the soil to take the seeds.
- Plant the seeds.
- Nourish the seedlings.
- Replant the seedlings into bigger, individual pots, then into the soil.
- Protect young plants from diseases and pests.
- Prune, water and fertilise them regularly.
- Enjoy the fruits of your labour.

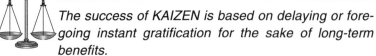

STRATEGY

Konosuke Matsushita is the founder of Matsushita Electric Company, one of the fifty largest corporations in the world. Matsushita's products are sold under the brand names of Panasonic, National, Technics and Quasar. He developed a long-term strategic plan for the company comprising ten phases. The plan itself spans 250 (!) years, with each phase lasting 25 years.

Repetition

"Zen is not some kind of excitement, but concentration on our usual everyday routine."

Shunryu Suzuki

The value of repetition is particularly obvious in new situations, when new concepts, ideas or methods have to be "connected' to the existing knowledge. Repetition helps us to establish the novelty and then connect it to what we already know, thereby forming a bonding relationship, a connection through repetition.

Routine does not have to be boring, uneventful or static. Repeating certain actions, thoughts and procedures is not the same as the drudgery of inappropriate, boring or unnecessary tasks.

Naturally, repetition can be both productive and counterproductive. Losers repeat mistakes, futile rituals, and actions that have stopped bringing the benefits they once did. Champions repeat actions that produce desired results, methods that work, thoughts that explore and probe, bringing new benefits and acting as a blueprint for new actions.

 STRATEGY

We become what we repeatedly do. Repetition creates excellence, which is not just an event, but a habit.

Rites And Rituals

"Any serious attempt to try to do something worthwhile is ritualistic."

Derek Walcott

Rituals help us to comprehend the intangible and transform it into the tangible. Concepts, ideas, motives, ideals, commitment and other elusive notions are easily communicated and reinforced through rites, symbols and rituals so comprehension of examples and actions gradually leads to understanding of broader concepts.

Rituals facilitate social interchanges and provide a common ground for discussion and analysis. Church groups, political parties, secret societies, sport and social clubs are some of the highly ritualised structures. Eric Berne, the author of *Games People Play* defines ritual as "a stereotyped series of simple complementary transactions programmed by external social forces."[6]

The value of rituals is their relative safety and predictability. Many occur between people who don't know each other well, so it serves to establish a common ground and helps them connect to each other and form initial bonds.

Many rituals change with the passage of time, and often lose their efficiency and practical usefulness. The only aspect that remains once their procedural validity is lost is their value as acts of faith.

Masaaki Imai also emphasises the importance of rituals in constant improvement: "Such things as sharing, caring and commitment are important in KAIZEN. Just as various rituals are needed in religion, KAIZEN also requires rituals, since people need ways to share their experiences, support one another, and build commitment together."[7]

Probably the most obvious ritual that can be observed in many companies in Japan is the reciting of slogans at various functions and gatherings ("A little better every day"; "Committed to people, committed to the future"; "Good thinking, good products"; "Constantly search for a better way") and the singing of company songs at the beginning of every working day.

 STORY

"But if you come at just any time, I shall never know at what hour my heart is to be ready to greet you. One must observe the proper rites."

"What is a rite?" asked the little prince.

"Those also are actions too often neglected," said the fox. "They are what make one day different from other days, one hour different from other hours. There is a rite, for example, among my hunters. Every Thursday they dance with the village girls. So Thursday is a wonderful

day for me! I can take a walk as far as the vineyards. But if the hunters danced at just any time, every day would be like every other day, and I should never have any vacation at all."[8]

3

Using The Right Tools For Continuous Improvement

RECIPE

Techniques are the ways of using various tools for maximising the benefits which come as a result of such use. The techniques of KAIZEN are:

- *Simplification – the process of systematic reduction of complex issues, problems and concepts down to a number of related simple entities.*

- *Transformation – the transfer of ideas, applications and techniques from one environment, area of life or product to the other.*

- *Visioning – projecting yourself into both the immediate and distant future, predicting change and anticipating possibilities for improvement.*

- *Recycling – the conservation and reuse of one's limited resources, finding new uses for old ideas.*

Self-Improvement Tools And Techniques

"Without tools man is nothing, with tools he is all."
Thomas Carlyle

Most things that lead to success are risky, scary and uncomfortable. To become a master of self-improvement takes intelligence (to understand the importance of it), courage (to take action and try new things) and persistence (to make continuous improvement work).

There are four basic groups of self-improvement tools:

- **Your internal (intangible) resources**
  (commitment, credibility, creativity, inquisitiveness, persistence, empathy, resourcefulness).

- **Your material (tangible) resources**
  (health, physical ability, space, time, money, material, possessions, investments).

- **Information**
  (general and specialist knowledge, experience, intelligence, expertise, facts, data).

- **Support**
  (moral and material support from others: mentors, friends, relatives, business circles).

Concentration

"The one prudence in life is concentration; the one evil is dissipation."
Ralph Waldo Emerson

We all discover concentration very early in life, but somehow forget its importance later. Like a child with a magnifying lens that can focus the sun's rays and start a fire, you too can focus your thoughts and efforts towards achieving our goals.

The principle is very simple: don't scatter your shots. When you set out to do something, do it, and do it straight away. Don't think about other things or problems while you are doing it. Filter your thoughts, especially the negative ones, which may distract you from your course.

Concentrate on your mission and stay committed to it until you accomplish your goals. Then move on, and concentrate your efforts on the next issue.

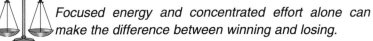

STRATEGY

Focused energy and concentrated effort alone can make the difference between winning and losing.

Focusing your actions, efforts and attention is the most powerful manifestation of commitment. It is more important to success than brilliance or intelligence.

Commitment

"According to the theory of aerodynamics, the bumblebee, because of its size, weight, and shape in relation to the total wingspread, should be unable to fly. But the bumblebee, being ignorant of these scientific truths, goes ahead and flies anyway."
Sign in a General Motors plant

In KAIZEN, a commitment to improvement is genuine and strong. Loose or conditional commitment is not a commitment. It's wishful thinking.

Continuous self-improvement seldom calls for a significant investment of money, but it does require a significant effort, commitment and will power, coupled with the investment in time. The good news is that once you choose KAIZEN and begin your quest for improvement, you are more likely to welcome the results and to stick with the self-improvement programme.

 STORY

A visitor to the zoo, fascinated by a huge elephant, noticed that the elephant was tied to a concrete pole with a tiny piece of chain that could easily be broken. "How can such a small chain prevent the elephant from breaking away?" he asked the zoo keeper.

"You see, sir," the keeper replied, "when this elephant was just a little baby, not bigger in size than you or me, we put it on a strong and heavy chain. He tried many times to get away, but he learned he couldn't. As he grew up, we used smaller and smaller chains. He quit trying. Now he simply looks down, sees the chain and never tries to pull on it."

Visioning

"Some men see things as they are and say, 'Why?'. I dream things that never were and say, 'Why not?'."

George Bernard Shaw

Visioning is the ability to predict, imagine and comprehend the future, and to use that vision in constructing your life and lives of others. Vision creates actions, commitment and a sense of responsibility. It enables you to anticipate, predict and act on that information, before it becomes obvious to others. Therefore, vision gives you an enormous competitive edge. Vision facilitates proactive efforts. Being proactive means acting before we are acted upon, trying to prevent events from happening, instead of merely reacting to them.

Being proactive may be difficult in times of change, uncertainty and unpredictability, just as are the times we live in. Instead of being proactive, you may have to be interactive, to interact with changes that will keep happening, most of which will be beyond your control or sphere of influence. What is within the powers of your control and under your direct influence is how you interact with those changes.

Visioning does not, as some say, hinder the ability to deal with and pay attention to details. On the contrary, by helping you to get the basics right it leaves you with more time and opportunity to sort the details out as well. It helps you to become the architect of your own future.

Living In The Right Time Zone

"And what I pity in you is something human,
The old incurable untimeliness,
Only begetter of all ills that are."
Robert Frost

There are three main time zones we could live in: the past, the present and the future. When I say "live in" what I really mean is that we are primarily oriented towards one of them. Some people live in the past: they are the "If only..." or "It might have been..." people. Some live for the present: they are the "now" people, who don't care much what's going to happen tomorrow. Others live solely for the future, sacrificing and hoping that the future will bring them success – that somehow the lucky break will happen: they are the "One day..." people.

KAIZEN is about living in the present tense, but preparing and actively building a future. This is where a critical difference lies between KAIZEN and "The power of positive thinking" philosophy. Positive mental attitude is necessary for success, there is no doubt about that. But thinking positively and having the right attitude is not enough for success. Unless such an attitude is coupled with a consistent, realistic, sound philosophy of improvement based on effort, knowledge and integrity, positive thinking is mere daydreaming. It is incomplete. What is missing are KAIZEN values.

Although KAIZEN lives in the present and works towards improving the future, both immediate and distant, its roots are in the past. Just as a tree grows in the present, reaches the sky (the future) and has its roots deeply in the soil from where it grew from (the past), the roots of your self-improvement have to be in the past. The past tells you which actions yielded positive results, which didn't, what worked, what didn't and what the difference was. The aim is to learn the lessons from the past.

Credibility

There is a magic word that opens many doors. That word is trust. To get cooperation from people, you have to win their trust. To delegate tasks and assume leadership, you need their trust. In fact, whatever you want to do – move up the corporate ladder, get a job at the interview, get a rise, a promotion or anything else – you should make people trust you. People feel comfortable with you and can relate to you if they trust you, and trust comes from two basic sources. One is competence, the other credibility.

Credibility is gained by keeping promises, appointments and by doing what you preach. You become credible if you live your philosophy and put words into action. The credibility gap is the difference between what you say and what you do.

ACTION

Always do what you promised you would do. Close that credibility gap. In other words, do what you preach.

Inquisitiveness

"I keep six honest serving men
They taught me all I knew:
Their names are What and Why and When
And How and Where and Who."
Rudyard Kipling

Information is power. No matter what you do – possess it, control it or create it – relevant and accurate information helps you make the right decisions, choose the right options and communicate in the right manner. Information may sometimes be thrown upon you, but in most cases you'll have to find it yourself.

Inquisitiveness is a quality that is developed very early in our lives, yet, for various reasons, as we grow older it levels off and then takes a dive. Yes, we tend to become complacent, we think we know it all, and what a big mistake we make. Ignorance is strength, says the government as it keeps its taxpayers in the dark, wasting funds and destroying the future. Ignorance is strength, says the employer as he keeps his employees in the dark, uninformed, fearful for their jobs, their existence. The course of action is obvious: don't be ignorant. Inquisitiveness is the first step towards mastery. If you don't possess it, acquire it. If you do, develop it further. Increase your level of inquisitiveness to a level of an average child and you'll be doing well. The removal of ignorance is best accomplished by exposure to books. Read.

Don't stop at being inquisitive. Go one step further: question authority. Don't take anything for granted; people, positions, power bases, procedures, protocols, pecking order. Try them on and see what stuff are they made of. Throw in a challenge. See where you stand in comparison to others. Just for trying, you'll win many points.

 REFLECTION

From the self-improvement point of view, 'Why?' is the most important word in any language. All knowledge, wisdom and achievement has its root in that simple syllable.

4

Implementing The Philosophy Of Constant Improvement

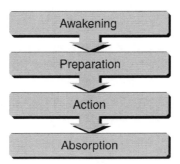

Figure 5. The four phases of improvement.

Awakening And Anticipation – The First Phase

"New ages are born so quietly that the majority of people are not aware of what is happening."

Bishop Gerald Kennedy

Self-improvement starts with awareness that comes as a result of awakening – recognising one's weaknesses and strong points, being aware of one's interactions with the environment and others, knowing what one's comparative advantages are and how to explore those advantages for maximum return. Anticipation is founded on awareness. It involves thinking, analysing, trend-watching and preparing for the changes and developments ahead.

Anticipation is about preparing oneself for the future, for meeting the demands imposed on us and those we impose on ourselves as a result of our self-improvement efforts. Instead of losing direction and becoming lost in daily trivialities and details, postponing actions through vague procrastination and forgoing advantages brought by one's skills, talents and personality, anticipation is not merely trying to keep up with developments, but actively visioning the future and preparing for it. Rather than waiting for things to happen and allowing oneself to be overwhelmed by the future, winners in all spheres of life anticipate and shape their own futures and identify the opportunities that lie ahead.

Anticipation is a feed-forward attitude. While feedback methods respond to changes that have already taken place, therefore always lagging behind and never eliminating the cause of the disturbance, feed-forward living involves anticipation of those disturbances and either preventing the preventable ones by swift and decisive actions or adjusting to the unpreventable ones before they take place, therefore maintaining balance at most times.

ACTION

Replace feedback thinking with feed-forward thinking.

Preparation – The Second Phase

"If I had eight hours to chop down a tree, I'd spend six sharpening my axe."

Abraham Lincoln

The preparation phase consolidates one's knowledge, feelings and resources. One of its main goals is the development of the skills you will need in the action phase. To prepare is to build confidence, facilitate learning and encourage creativity and resourcefulness.

While the awakening phase tries to come to terms with the need for change and improvement and anticipation tries to predict, analyse and plan for the future but doesn't take any actions about it, the preparation phase is based on the acceptance of the often shocking realisation that something has to be done. The emotions are channelled into positive outlets: the frustration and fears so widely and abundantly present in the awakening phase are soothed out and harnessed to help focusing into the new direction.

The aim of preparation is to disturb the status quo and to pave the road towards the things to come. This phase is more organised and controlled than the first one, which is almost always chaotic and very often confusing .

Action – The Third Phase

"In a life where death is the hunter, my friend, there is no time for fear or regrets – only decisions."
Carlos Castaneda, *Tales of Power*

The action phase is the first to bring immediate results, simply because problems and issues get immediate attention. Those immediate results are not the primary aim of KAIZEN (the continuity of purpose and actions is) but they play an important role as motivators. They generate enthusiasm and create that initial impetus needed for change.

QUESTION

Think about all the actions you have taken recently. What are the most significant practical self-improvement steps you have made?

These are some of the most important practical self-improvement steps I have taken in the last twelve months:

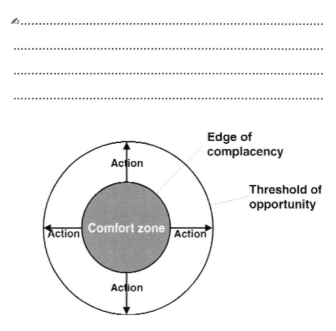

Figure 7. Actions close the gap between our comfort zones and
thresholds of opportunity.

Absorption And Consolidation – The fourth Phase

Absorption is the period for reflection and analysis. This is the time
to evaluate the actions taken in the action phase and the results of those
actions. It is also the time to reflect on the past, the present and the
future, to get an accurate overview of the cause-and-effect relationships within one's continuous improvement. Absorption and reflection
ensure that current and oncoming opportunities are not missed, but
seized and capitalised upon, that alternatives are considered and the
best possible paths chosen.

Absorption deals with six basic descriptors of every action, every improvement step, every achievement or setback. These six descriptors could be formulated in many different ways, but their shortest form is that of the questions WHO, WHEN, WHERE, WHAT, WHY and HOW. There is nothing in this world that cannot be accurately and completely described if the answers to those six questions are found.

The six basic questions may be asked in many ways and applied to any aspect of continuous improvement. In terms of monitoring your progress and achievements, but also setbacks and difficulties, the first and most basic question is: "Does the philosophy of KAIZEN serve my interests best?" Then you may expand on it by asking: "Is KAIZEN my deliberate choice or simply a fad that appeals to me or some transient feeling?" Many more reflections should regularly take place during your absorption phase:

 ### *REFLECTION*

Is my approach methodical enough? Have I devised a system that will, when put into practice, maximise the benefits of self-improvement and minimise the losses?

How do I feel about my improvement efforts and the whole KAIZEN philosophy?

Am I satisfied with my progress so far?

What could I do to speed it up or achieve more in a given time?

Consolidation is focused on maintaining the momentum and the benefits of continuous improvement. Its primary concern is the maintenance of things achieved and providing plateaux from which new endeavours are undertaken.

People who treat continuous improvement purely as a motivational tool never reach the consolidation stage. They get lost searching for shortcuts and gambits that could bring them immediate gratification and quick results without a genuine involvement and integrated approach to improvement.

5

Managing Change

Make Yourself Into A Champion

DEFINITION

Champions ....

...set goals that are neither to easy nor too difficult to attain. They prefer moderately challenging tasks. Easy tasks, when carried out successfully, would not provide the sense of achievement. Difficult tasks leave them open to failure.

...need a constant feedback on how they are doing. That feedback comes from three sources: from the task itself, from others and from their own perception of their success.

...keep a record of their wins and loses, their track record. This helps them to constantly monitor and analyse their performance.

...look for tasks that can provide them with a sense of personal responsibility and accountability, providing they have control over them and the ultimate decision-making power and authority.

...rely on personal and collective effort. They avoid gambling situations and don't want to depend on luck or other factors beyond their control.

...are not power-driven. They are achievement-driven. Achievement is what they seek and what they live for.... take action. They don't wait for conditions to be perfect, because they know they never will be.

...respond to change instead of reacting to it. They choose the most appropriate response, so it brings the maximum benefit.

...manage, lead, motivate and deploy themselves. They do not allow others to manage or deploy them to fight for someone else's cause. They are focused on their own cause.

...prepare themselves, so they are ready to take the advantage of the opportunities that lie ahead.

...possess a positive, balanced attitude towards life, coupled with inquisitiveness, persistence, stamina and resourcefulness.

...don't overestimate their strengths and underestimate their weaknesses. They have a realistic view of their assets and liabilities.

...intentionally and deliberately push themselves out of their comfort zones, over the threshold of opportunity and away from the edge of complacency.

Some call them high achievers, others relate to them as the winners. The most accurate term would probably be champions. A champion doesn't necessarily always win, and doesn't always achieve some high goal. Champions are simply worthwhile, resourceful, consistent persons, who follow their inner drive for constant improvement and have a mission in life, no matter how simple or profound it may be. Champions set goals and make their own rules. They also set their own standards for evaluating their performance and devise their own reward systems for rewarding the achievements.

Champions realise that the skills, knowledge and drive for success are the qualities that are going to make them great, and that those attributes can be intensified, fortified and synergetically combined through constant self-improvement strategy and effort. They are not afraid to make that effort.

Becoming a champion is a continuous process of designing and redesigning yourself. Planning, implementing and evaluating are phases of an overall design process. Designing your life is one such process.

Embrace Uncertainty, Unpredictability And Ambiguity

"Two things seemed pretty apparent to me. One was, that in order to be a pilot[9] a man had got to learn more than any one man ought to be allowed to know; and the other was that he must learn it all over again in a different way every 24 hours."
Mark Twain, *Life on the Mississippi*

People, organisations and institutions thrive on certainty, predictability and safety. Uncertainty and surprises make them less powerful, even vulnerable. Once taken out of their comfort zones, feelings of complacency, satisfaction, dominance and power are replaced by fear, uneasiness, panic, helplessness. Guerrilla fighters know that, and subsequently base their tactics on these very premises – surprise, uncertainty, unpredictability.

The current educational and organisational system that prevails in the Western world is heavily oriented towards logical, structural thinking and places emphasis on methods and aims which require the removal of uncertainty, ambiguity and unpredictability. Individual and corporate life is seldom rational, structured and logical.

The ability to deal with possibilities, intuitive concepts, feelings and paradoxes of modern age is gaining in importance in the organisational arena, although the educational system still has to come to terms with the requirements for broader, less rigid and structured training and education.

Learn To Live With Incompleteness And Imperfection

"There is a time in every man's education when he arrives at the conviction that envy is ignorance, that imitation is suicide, that he must take himself for better or worse as his portion; that though the wide universe is full of good, no kernel of nourishing corn can come to him but through the toil bestowed on that plot of ground which is given to him to till. The power which resides in him is new in nature, and none but he knows what that is which he can do, nor does he know until he has tried... Trust thyself: every heart vibrates to that iron string."
Ralph Waldo Emerson, *Self-Reliance*

A human being, just as any other product or form of life, is never complete and perfect. A state of incompleteness and imperfection is a natural state, which lends itself to the concept of improvement, modification, refinement and advancement. Incompleteness symbolises unfulfilled and unrealised possibilities and future opportunities. It encourages you to develop new ideas and find new applications for the old ones.

Accepting your own imperfections and flaws, your lack of certain skills and qualities is the first step towards improvement. It should not be seen as a sign of weakness and inadequacy, but as an opportunity for achievement. That opportunity should be embraced and capitalised on.

The concept of incompleteness (*mikansei*) has been an underlying concept of art and etiquette in Japan. Unfulfilled possibilities which elicit creative responses through the use of imagination and refinement are everywhere, from minimalist brush strokes on a canvas and short *haiku* poetry to the asymmetric and minimalist flower arrangements and Japanese gardens.

In the corporate sector, employers, under the notion of *mikansei*, encourage their employees to develop new ideas and keep refining, modifying and polishing the old ones. Old products, seen as "incomplete", are often enhanced through the addition of new features which make them highly desirable to consumers and result in hot sales. You can see how KAIZEN fits perfectly into incompleteness – constant improvement and refinement is a never-ending process, a window into future opportunities.

> **DEFINITION**
>
> **Mikansei** *is the Japanese orientation towards incompleteness, which is seen not as an imperfection, but primarily as an opportunity for improvement and constant refinement.*

Become The Master Of Change

"Success in life begins with acceptance. Accept the things that can't be changed or are perhaps too difficult to change. Then start to change the one thing you have control over. Yourself."
Al Ries and Jack Trout, *Horse Sense (The key to success is finding a horse to ride)*

Change is a dual concept. It can be both beneficial and detrimental. When the change is imposed on us, we feel at its mercy. We feel threatened by uncertainty, instability, uprooting, turbulence, discomfort, confusion. When change originates outside our sphere of influence, we feel it as something imposed, something others use to control us and dictate their terms and conditions. Imposed change usually results in a loss of security and confidence.

When change is the product of our efforts, when we are active participants in bringing change about, when it's done by us, for our own benefit and as a result of fulfilling our needs, change is one of the highest achievements of an individual or an organisation. While the old form of security, based on control of one's destiny and one's resources, is a victim of imposed change, a new form of security, based on flexibility and discovering new tools, is developed through self-produced change.

Rosabeth Moss Canter, in her famous book *The Change Masters*, summarises well when she says:

"The individuals who will succeed and flourish will also be masters of change: adept at reorienting their own and others' activities in untried directions to bring about higher levels of achievement. They will be able to acquire and use power to produce innovation."[10]

 FURTHER READING: The Strategy of the Dolphin

The subtitle of this unorthodox work by Dudley Lynch and Paul Kordis is the best description of what this book is all about: "Scoring a win in a chaotic world."

The metaphor of the dolphin symbolises a new frontier in thinking and responding to challenges of the future. It breaks away from the myths of the shark (winning at any cost), the carp (avoiding losses) and the pseudo-enlightened carp (settle for a win/win situation as soon as possible, despite the fact that it doesn't meet the needs of either side). The strategy of the dolphin is the strategy for applying KAIZEN to constantly accelerating change. Read this book.(D. Lynch and P.L. Kordis, William Morrow and Company, New York, 1988).

Maintain The Momentum Of Change

"Perhaps the most valuable result of all education is the ability to make yourself do the thing you have to do when it ought to be done, whether you like it or not; it is the first lesson that ought to be learned; and however early a man's training begins, it is probably the last lesson that he learns thoroughly."

Thomas Huxley

Successful self-management is based on two pillars. One is self-improvement, the other is maintenance. While improvement relates to improving your standards, resources and the ways you do things, maintenance encompasses all activities directed towards maintaining those standards, resources and activities, preventing them from slipping back to old, inferior ways of thinking, doing, achieving and living.

Maintenance is based on constant education, self-discipline and practice. Only by using your faculties and skills will you maintain your proficiency, fluency and responsiveness to situations. To keep achieving new plateaux and raising your standards, you have to keep consolidating your position and achieved levels.

Maintaining the momentum of change is becoming an increasingly demanding activity. The pace of change is accelerating, there is less and less time for responding to its challenges, for learning and application of the knowledge gained. The plateaux reached and used for consolidation are shorter and more frequent.

Establishing cause-effect linkages is a crucial activity in the process of managing change. Changing too frequently can disrupt those causal relationships and eliminate the learning benefit of the changes made. It is of vital importance to allow enough time for the changes to consolidate and their impact to become evident, otherwise it will not be known if the changes made produced desired effects or not.

DEFINITION

KAIZEN is synchronism between sensing, feeling, thinking, doing, being, improving, taking, giving, managing, relating and planning.

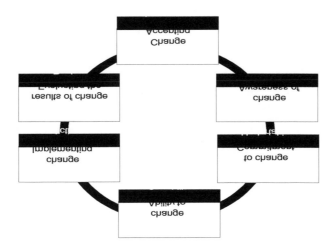

Figure 8. The change circle: change as a continuous process

Do Whatever Comes Naturally

"If you follow your bliss, you put yourself on a kind of track, which has been there all the while waiting for you, and the life that you ought to be living is the one you are living."

Joseph Campbell

Our minds and bodies know what is best for us. They feel it; we sometimes don't. Self-improvement is basically about doing what is best for you in the best way possible. Imperfections, inadequacies, sickness, flaws, inferior performance and living beyond one's capabilities often result from obstructing, denying or ignoring what is best for you. Natural, sound and sensible living calls for natural, sound and sensible improvement, which will enable you to maximise your natural potential and benefit from them. Achieving something by sacrificing your physical and mental resources and by impeding nature in or around yourself is a Pyrrhic victory, if it could be called a victory at all. It will eventually lead to a great loss and an ultimate defeat.

REFLECTION

Losers dwell on their limitations; champions focus on their opportunities.

Natural talents and playfulness go well together. Play was the first path of learning for ancient cultures and has always been the primary source of knowledge for children, who play with objects, images, concepts and ideas, combining them and relating them to each other. As a form of mostly subconscious mental activity which comes naturally to them, such playfulness should be nurtured and maintained in adults, who seldom learn just by random messing around and exploring without a master-goal or definite aim.

It is possible that too much of a focus on certain goals and aims prevents adults from seeing other possibilities, opportunities and alternative ways of learning and achieving.

Develop A Powerful Mindsight

"If you can see in any given situation only what everybody else can see, you can be said to be so much a representative of your culture that you are a victim of it."

S. I. Hayakawa

The actions you took in the past, have been taking presently or will take in the future determine the quality of that future. They will increase the importance of the future and its influence over your past and present alike. The past cannot be altered: it can only serve as a guidepost to the future.

To succeed in your self-actualisation and self-improvement efforts, you need a dream. A great dream is what makes life great – it is a starting point to every achievement. To develop your dream and to put it into practice, you also need a powerful mindsight. A mindsight is the ability to see things not just as they are (the power to see things as they are is called eyesight), but to see them as they could be.

78

How successfully you use your mindsight will determine how successful you'll be in your self-improvement. Mindsight is not wishing or daydreaming. It is creating mental pictures of your own future and transforming those images into reality through consistent, methodical, concentrated effort and determination.

RECIPE

Be ready for the future. Anticipate and predict. See possibilities before they become obvious.

6

Applying KAIZEN To Problem Solving

Recognise Your Problems And The Need To Solve Them

"It is only because of problems that we grow mentally and spiritually. It is through the pain of confronting and resolving problems that we learn."

M. Scott Peck

All problem-solving starts with the recognition that every individual or corporation has problems and that problems are a normal and natural part of everyday life. Without problems there would be no KAIZEN, there would be no self-improvement. The notion that only unsuccessful people have problems is dangerous and false. The only people without any problems whatsoever are those in cemeteries.

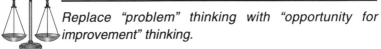

STRATEGY

Replace "problem" thinking with "opportunity for improvement" thinking.

KAIZEN is therefore a problem-solving process, too. Improvement stems from recognising the need for improvement by recognising and admitting to oneself that problems exist. Complacency, suppressing negative issues within oneself, procrastination, wishful thinking and other ways of avoiding facing problems and other issues are all enemies of KAIZEN.

Once the initial stage of recognising and accepting problems is over, KAIZEN provides indications on how to deal with them in a systematic and thorough manner, through the use of various problem-solving tools.

Recognising problems and imperfections and shortcomings is far from easy. Most people gradually develop a kind of functional blindness to their own defects and shortcomings. This is probably the main cause of their inability to resolve the problems they face – not because those problems are difficult and cannot be overcome, but simply because they are not seen!

ACTION

All problems are like a black box. Open yours and investigate them inside out. Take them into pieces and put them back together. Change them as many times as you can. Keep yourself challenged and enthusiastic about finding solutions.

Minimise Delays

The continuous improvement circle (illustrated in Figure 9) has three major milestones. It starts with a perceived need for improvement, which ultimately (after an "action delay") leads to some kind of action designed and applied in order to rectify the situation. So the first step is geared towards the rectification of a problem, resolution of a situation, attainment of goals, avoidance of loss or improvement of performance.

The delay between a realisation that improvement is possible and/or needed and the taking of appropriate action could conveniently be called an action delay. An "active" component of that delay is the time needed to study the situation or an issue, to devise a plan of action and to "engineer" the solution. Other components of the action delay are "reactive". Procrastination and wishful thinking are just some of the possible reasons for the counterproductive delays.

Once the actions are taking place, however, the results of those actions may not become evident until later in the process. This is known as a "manifestation delay"; it takes some time for the results of the actions to manifest themselves and become noticeable, observable and measurable. When people or organisations abandon their course of action or change it prematurely (before any significant improvements could be noticed), the manifestation delay is often the main culprit.

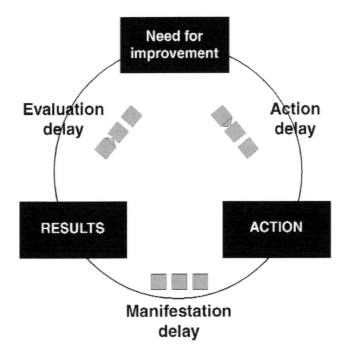

Figure 9. The "delay" circle.

As soon as the first results became evident, the evaluation process should start to take place. Its aim is to introduce corrective actions if deemed necessary and to reassess the newly-created situation, i.e.. to re-evaluate the new need for improvement (if any). Once the proper evaluation system is in place and the habit of evaluation has been created, the self-controlled mechanism of the feedback improvement loop sustains itself in a quite stable manner.

The main reason for "overdoing it" (taking actions to far for too long in a too strong manner) is the postponement of such evaluative practice, which could often create a need for new corrective actions that have to be introduced to neutralise the adverse results of the original improvement effort.

ACTION

• *Action delay leads to problems getting worse, situations deteriorating, issues becoming clouded.*

• *Manifestation delay leads to false thinking that corrective actions do not work or do not work as they should.*

• *Evaluation delay leads either to "overdoing it" (if too much corrective action was applied) or to the creation of an unknown situation where those involved do not know the results of their actions.*

Search For Flexible Solutions

Your attitude towards problems will determine how successful you'll be in solving them. Champions are sensitive both to problems caused by others and to problems whose causes lie within themselves. Losers are sensitive to the problems caused by others but are not able or willing to see those problems they've created themselves.

There are three ways an individual or an organisation may deal with a problem:

• *Ignore it and hope it will go away.* This is obviously the initial reaction in many cases. It's like hoping that everything is just a bad dream and that it will somehow all be gone in the morning. Miracles of that kind seldom happen in real life. Ignorance is a weakness and the results are always negative. What you don't know and things you don't do can and will hurt you. Eliminate this option from your problem-solving list.

- *Respond to it in a systematic and resourceful manner.* Responding is a prudent practice. While reacting is often a disorganised, hit-and-miss approach, it can be a planned, well-thought-out and appropriate action. Reacting is based on contingency and crisis plans which provide blueprints for dealing with problems, crises and adversities.

- *Predict it and try to prevent it from occurring.* Now we are talking about being proactive, instead of reactive or responsive. This advanced stage of the problem-solving attitude is about monitoring trends, setting standards and early spotting of deviations and anomalies that could (at an early stage) be resolved much more easily than when they turn into bigger issues and become significant problems later.

Solutions KAIZEN style are never fixed, absolute or final. Flexibility and responsiveness call for relational solutions, which relate not only to problems, but also to the contexts in which those problems appear and to the specifics of the owner of the problem. Those specifics reflect your particular situation – your profession, personality, character and environment as well as your financial, emotional and spiritual state.

This pragmatism of solutions creates a balance between goals and objectives that are implemented through action-based solutions to problems and the constraints of current situation. Since both objectives and constraints change continuously, it is obvious that solutions and actions have to change accordingly to be effective and appropriate.

STRATEGY

KAIZEN rules for effective problem-solving:

• *Problems are treasure-bearing mountains that surround us. Dig for that treasure.*

• *Seek problems relentlessly and vigorously. Don't shy away.*

• *Distinguish between symptoms and real causes. Don't try to cure the symptoms; cure or remove the cause and the symptoms will also disappear.*

• *Be problem-conscious, always on a lookout for new problems, new opportunities for improvement.*

• *Classify problems. Group them together and compare them. Stratification and classification are powerful tools that lead to better understanding.*

Use "Bricolage"

Claude Levi-Strauss, the French anthropologist, coined a term *bricolage* to describe the thought patterns and learning processes of "primitive" societies. *Bricolage* is based on irrational, intuitive, inductive reasoning, based on experimenting with various possibilities and variables in search for improved combinations, solutions to problems and configurations of systems.

Bricoleurs are wizards of intuition who mess around with solutions, using available resources, and search for pragmatic premises on which to base their future actions. Although this often means acting without a clear, detailed and definite sense and understanding of situations and future developments, *bricoleurs* are always on a lookout for possible improvements, seeking pragmatic solutions and answers through inductive reasoning and guidance from their daily experiences.

DEFINITION

Bricoleur: *One who explores possibilities, plays with resources, randomly tinkers with concepts and objects, and learns about mutual dependencies and relationships in order to arrive at workable solutions without a structured plan.*

Change Your Spectacles

Dealing with issues, life's problems, choices and opportunities requires adaptability and relativity. Stewardship, which we defined as a strategic use of resources, also demands a holistic approach, where all aspects of a certain situation, issue or problem are considered and their mutual relationships are exposed.

• *Pragmatic and conservative*

Emphasises routines and formal ways; recognises structures and patterns; considers formal, routine, procedural and administrative aspects of situations and issues; tries to keep in control of the situation; judges by evaluating practical consequences and applications.

• *Analytical and logical*

Gathers facts and figures; obtains as much information as possible; looks for leads and clues; follows and analyses trends; follows vertical thinking patterns; comprehensive and neutral point of view; non-judgemental and detached; looks rationally at the situation.

• *Intuitive and impressionistic*

Builds hypothesis and theories; high value placed on initial impressions and hunches; looks at the whole and explores the general, overall feeling it evokes.

• *Creative and innovative*

Explores lateral thinking; looks for new way of doing things; considers doing things differently, doing different things at different times, for different reasons, by using different tools.

• *Sensory and emotional*

Sensitive, in tune with surroundings; concerned about human side of issues; understanding others, their views, values and actions; considers interpersonal aspects and implications; searches for feelings, influence, persuasion, conciliation.

QUESTION

"Two men look out through the same bars:
One sees the mud, and one the stars."
Frederick Langbridge,
A Cluster of Quiet Thoughts

This is my favourite verse. What would your verse be?

Recognise And Appreciate Beauty

"We ascribe beauty to that which is simple; which has no superfluous parts; which exactly answers its end; which stands related to all things; which is the mean of many extremes."
Ralph Waldo Emerson, *The Conduct of Life*

Beauty is both a tool and a consequence. As a tool of the designer (and we have seen that we are all designers of our lives, our relationships and our environment), beauty and aesthetics help us shape both our inner world and that around us into objects and concepts that inspire and move, please and intrigue, excite and compel to act.

In his book *Design For The Real World*, Victor Papanek concludes: "Because there is no ready yardstick for the analysis of aesthetics, it is simply considered to be a personal expression fraught with mystery."

As a consequence, beauty stems from the roots of our thoughts and actions. Striving for betterment and proficiency of skills and thoughts directly lead to elegance and simplicity. How many times have you admired a perfection brought to the point of ultimate elegance and simplicity while watching beautiful, elegant ballerinas dance or gymnasts perform on various devices? Who hasn't admired smooth lines of a shell or praised the diligence and organisational skills of bees, admired the easy and beauty of seagull's flight? Elegance and beauty come from proficiency, from the mastering of one's craft, one's purpose, oneself.

 STORY

Richard Fuller, the reputable architect and engineer, was once asked by one of his students if he thought about aesthetic aspects when reaching decisions on technical problems. "No. When I'm working on a problem, I never think about beauty. I only think of how to solve the problem. But when I have finished, if the solution is not beautiful, I know it's wrong."

Develop Intellectual Curiosity

"We never stop investigating. We are never satisfied that we know enough to get by. Every question we answer leads on to another question. This has become the greatest survival trick of our species."
Desmond Morris, *The Naked Ape*

Curiosity is one of the most permanent and certain characteristics of a vigorous intellect. Curiosity is, in great and generous minds, the first passion and the last. The questions we ask determine everything we do in life, from our relationships to the careers we choose and the income we earn. The questions we ask others and ourselves, directly or indirectly, shape our destiny. The questions we don't want to ask, don't know how to ask or are afraid of asking shape our destiny even more.

The quality of the questions we ask determines the quality of our lives. People who ask better questions, and those who ask the right questions more often than others, get better answers. Those answers help them to get to know themselves and others better.

The right questions are crucial if you want to find the right answers. The right answers are useless if you keep answering the wrong questions.

Questions help us break through our self-imposed limitations and to evaluate life's options. Questions have the power to immediately shift our focus and change our feelings. They empower us in moments of crisis and help us find what we are really about and why we do certain things the way we do.

 STORY

"What is the answer?" asked Gertrude Stein on her deathbed, wanting to know if the doctors had decided to operate on her. When the answer didn't come, she responded, "In that case, what is the question?"

- What are my alternatives? What are the pros and cons of each alternative?
- What developments could affect my mission?
- What knowledge and skills will I need to successfully complete my mission?
- Where and how do I acquire the knowledge and develop the skills needed?
- How will my choices affect my future?
- What are the critical factors of my success?
- How do I control and achieve those critical factors?
- Why do we do it this way?

- Does it make sense?
- Why should we change this?
- Why shouldn't we change this?
- Are there other, better ways of doing this?
- What are our competitors doing?
- What is the core problem?
- Is this a cause or a consequence?
- Who can help us solve this problem?
- What are we trying to achieve?
- How can we make this better, cheaper or in less time?
- Is this a good idea?
- What are the alternatives?
- Is this the right time/place/method?
- Are we reinventing the wheel? Has this been done before?
- Where is the opportunity? How do I recognise it and capitalise on it?
- What resources do I need and how to control them?
- Who can make this project work?
- What decisions have to be made?
- Who will be affected by those decisions?
- Where are we now and where are we going?
- How do we get there?
- What can go wrong and why?

Test Before You Act

"Test" is a word normally associated with formal education and therefore may have many negative connotations. You may remember your nervousness before an exam, your cramming or negative feeling associated with being evaluated by others. The truth is that testing is natural part of our lives. Testing is what we do on a regular and continuous basis. As we go through life and explore different options, we test those options. As we meet people we test them to see if they deserve our confidence or not – are they to be trusted and counted upon or otherwise?

One thing we unfortunately seldom do is test ourselves, which is a pity, because the surest way to improvement is through regular and relevant testing of your emotions, knowledge, methods, goals, assets and liabilities.

DEFINITION

Keep testing = keep improving; Stop testing = stop improving.

Testing is an integral part of a valuable problem-solving tool: scenario-building. Preparing scenarios of various outcomes and possibilities makes anticipating change and preparing for it easier and quicker.

Don't Hesitate To Change Your Mind

"Change and growth take place when a person has risked himself and dares to become involved with experimenting with his own life."

Herbert Otto

Every decision, once made, can be unmade; everything once decided can be undecided. You don't have to live with a bad decision, or with a sound decision based on bad judgement. All you have to do is change it.

The ability to experiment, learn from mistakes and think in a free and effective manner will prove to be of paramount importance in your self-improvement efforts. Throughout our lives, we are taught to avoid making mistakes, to play it safe and go quietly about our business. That's the most damaging school of thought one can attend. That rationale leaves us unprepared for failures in life and unable to capitalise on those temporary setbacks.

STRATEGY

Don't hesitate to change directions.

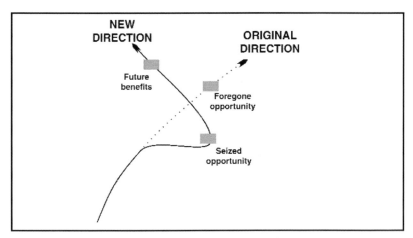

Figure 10. A permanent change of direction.

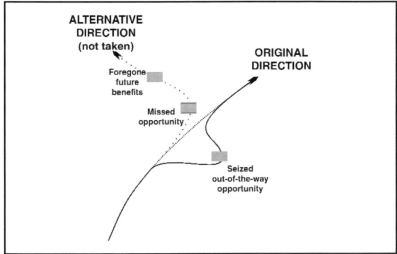

Figure 11. Temporary change to seize an out-of-the-way opportunity.

POEM

Two roads diverged in a yellow wood,
And sorry I could not travel both
And be one traveller, long I stood
And looked down as far as I could
To where it bent in the undergrowth;
Then took the other,as just as fair,
And having perhaps the better claim,
Because it was grassy and wanted wear;
Though as for the passing there
Had worn them really about the same,
And both that morning equally lay
In leaves no step had trodden back.
Oh, I kept the first for another day!
Yet knowing how way leads onto a way,
I doubted I should ever come back.
I shall be telling this with a sigh
Somewhere ages and ages hence:
Two roads diverged in a wood and I –
I took the one less travelled by.
And that has made all the difference.

Robert Frost, *The Road Not Taken*

Focus On Process, Not Just On Results

"The man who is aware of himself is henceforward independent; and he is never bored, and life is only too short, and he is steeped through and through with a profound yet temperate happiness. He alone lives, while other people, slaves of ceremony, let life slip past them in a kind of dream."

Virginia Woolf

The improvement of an individual or a corporation is not a simple matter of focusing on the desired end results and striving to achieve them, but also an ongoing improvement of the existing means and

93

ways to obtain those results and a never-ending quest for new, better ways to pursue one's goals. It is as much a process-oriented philosophy as it is a quest for results.

STRATEGY

Take care of the method: first improve the process, and the results will follow naturally and automatically.

Process orientation means paying attention to the ways one does things, performs tasks and organises one's resources. If those activities can be done better, faster, with less effort or without as much resources, then we say that the process is improved. Alternatively, if more results are obtained while using the same amount of resources, again, the process is more efficient. Almost everything individuals or corporations do in life can be looked at from this efficiency perspective, and can subsequently be improved.

As individuals, we are involved in processes as similar and as diverse as learning a foreign language, mastering a new skill, improving reading speed, finding a better job, raising a child, falling in love, enhancing one's self-esteem, shaping up for summer, etc.

In the corporate sector, processes are more obvious: manufacturing assembly lines, mining and mineral processing plants, maintenance procedures, serving pizza in a fast food outlet, restructuring and retraining of a work force.

When we talk about self-improvement, we talk about the improvement of our processes, of the ways we do certain things and of the speed we are moving towards our goals (results). We talk about the pursuit of more, better and faster. The results we get in life are direct consequences of processes that create those results. To get better results the processes have to be improved. To manage our resources better, we have to devise processes that will utilise those resources properly, without waste. To eliminate waste, the processes that create that waste have to be dealt with.

DEFINITION

KAIZEN focuses on improvement through process-oriented thinking, because the improvement of a process is a prerequisite for the achievement of worthwhile results.

7

Carving The Building Blocks Of Success

Realise That Success Is A Many-Splendoured Thing

"Outward success alienates a man from himself. Self-alienation, another name for self-ignorance, is the worst that can befall a man inasmuch as it leads to the loss of inner light and, inevitably, the loss of his vision altogether. A person's inability to see his way ahead makes him a prisoner within himself; it isolates him from everything outside the narrow entity of "self" and, therefore, annuls his belonging in humanity."

Anwar el-Sadat

In his autobiography[11], Anwar el-Sadat distinguishes between two types of success – inner and outer. To him, only inner success can maintain one's internal equilibrium, help a man to find his peace of mind and stay true to himself. Without being true to oneself, no man can be true to others. The outer success, which gets the attention of the media and is often stereotyped and portrayed in the movies, literature and art, is based on one's image, on how others perceive him, and, most importantly, on many circumstances beyond one's control.

Al Ries and Jack Trout, marketing gurus and authors of management classics such as *Positioning, Marketing Warfare* and *Bottom-up Marketing*, in their book on success, *Horse Sense*, give this definition of success:

> *"Success in life begins with acceptance. Accept the things that can't be changed or are perhaps too difficult to change. Than start to change the one thing you have total control over. Yourself."*

There is no words that could better summarise the essence of *KAIZEN and You*. That's it. If, after reading this book, you remember nothing else except that profound statement, you'd be doing fine.

DEFINITION
_____

Success is many things to many people and different things to different people.

Decide What Success Means To You

> *"I dread success. To have succeeded is to have finished one's business on earth, like the male spider, who is killed by the female the moment he has succeeded in courtship. I like a state of continual becoming, where the goal is in front, and not behind."*
> George Bernard Shaw

Measuring and analysing success is one of the main causes of frustration and misunderstanding for individuals and corporations. Success is a state of mind and it should be treated as such; it should be measured with feelings.

Because many individuals and corporations don't know how to manage success, managing and sustaining success can prove to be more difficult than achieving success. It requires different tools, methods and different style than achieving success. Frederick Herzberg summarises it well when he says:

"The major problem in our society is that we don't know how to manage success. Throughout history, the great tragedies of cultures or organisations have not been in the failure to produce success but in the failure to manage it once it's been achieved. Managing success needs a different managerial style than producing success."[12]

Individuals, as well as corporations, approach success in different ways and treat success differently. Some work hard for it, some achieve it with apparently little effort, but all have to manage it. Some don't want success at all. They are not prepared to make sacrifices and to put in the required effort. Fortunately, you don't belong to this category, otherwise you wouldn't be reading this book right now.

To achieve success through continuous improvement you have to think continuously about success: define it; visualise it; analyse it; feel it; become comfortable with it; accept and cherish it.

The boxes in Figure 12 define various aspects of our lives. Success can be achieved in any of those areas. Many people achieve no success in any of them. Others are successful in one or two areas and fail in others; their lives lack balance. Rare are the individuals who reach success in all of these facets of life.

Interestingly enough, no matter how many of these areas bring us success, most of us know what we want from each of them. Think about them carefully. Decide what improvements you want to make in each area and what ultimate goals you want to reach. Then write them in the boxes provided. Regularly review the improvements you have made and the goals those improvements may lead to. Make regular updates and changes as necessary.

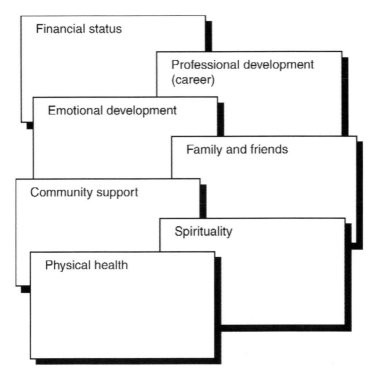

Figure 12. Define the meaning of success in all spheres of your life.

Create Your Own Strategies For Success

"If to petrify is success, all one has to do is to humor the lazy side of the mind: but if to grow is success, then one must wake up anew every morning and keep awake all day."

Henry Ford, *My Life and Work*[13]

Self-improvement is about creating one's own strategies for success, for one's own self-development and growth. Just as successful corporations create plans and strategies to reach their medium and long-term goals, individuals also have the power to search and find their own ways and methods of achieving and channelling their resources towards strategic aims.

Despite the time and effort of management which gets invested in planning, strategic thinking and defining what their business is all about, many corporations have serious problems in defining their mission, their values and strategies. These difficulties reflect directly into their success and profitability. Individuals are in even more serious position. Abandoned by the educational, religious and corporate systems (none of which has been successful in providing constructive and beneficial guidance and support), they are left to drift aimlessly, unable to consolidate their efforts and deploy their resources towards self-empowerment and self-development.

Without serious understanding of their values, goals, assets and inadequacies, they view life in terms of incoherent, short-term plans and goals, vague opinions and preconceived notions about both themselves and their environment.

In *KAIZEN and You* we talk about strategic self-improvement, strategic development of people and corporations. Strategic is a key word of the concept. It emphasises the importance and the value of effective strategies through which actions and resources are synergetically compounded towards success.

 FURTHER READING: *Horse Sense*

"The key to success is finding a horse to ride" is the one-line summary of this book wisdom. Al Ries and Jack Trout, marketing wizards and guerrilla fighters, know what life is all about and what it isn't. Trying harder, relying on yourself and thinking positively is not enough for success. What is needed is knowledge of which horse to ride, when to change horses and when to go from trotting to galloping. (A. Ries and J. Trout, McGraw-Hill, New York, 1991)

Accept And Cherish Success

"One is happy as a result of one's own efforts, once one knows the necessary ingredients of happiness: Simple tastes, a certain degree of courage, self-denial to a point, love of work, and above all, a clear conscience."

George Sand

Sooner or later, KAIZEN will bring success for you. Maybe you are already successful and want to reach new levels of achievement. In any case, to be a champion, you have to know how to handle success. It is a skill as important as the skill of becoming successful, because there is no point in becoming successful if you are not able to stay successful or if that success is only going to ruin you.

The society we live in presents us with numerous opportunities for success, although most are well hidden or not so obvious to our eyes and minds. The problem is in the way success is treated in society. Most people haven't yet realised how vital and how necessary success is to everyone. They haven't realised that they can be successful in any endeavour of their choice, if that successful attitude is encouraged in a mature, sensible way.

Mediocrity, jealousy and disbelief are all enemies of success. They are also impediments to self-improvement. Make the task of fostering and encouraging success and constant improvement your mission.

Do What Others Won't Do

"A craft can only have meaning when it serves a spiritual way."

Titus Burkhardt

One of the most important lessons in my life happened when I discovered that the fellow who was running a recycling yard was a millionaire. I was about ten years old and he was about forty. He had a cart and one horse and he drove through the suburbs of my home town shouting "I buy batteries, pipes, radiators, any metal, any shape, any size." I felt sorry for him. His image was an image of a poor man, of a scavenger of old, useless, unwanted objects that I associated with poverty and misery. Little did I realise the value of those items, which, if bought cheap and sold at a current market rate for lead, zinc, copper, aluminium or whatever metal he had (and he had them all), can realise a fortune. And that was exactly what happened.

To illustrate the concept further, I discovered the same about the guy who was selling fried pumpkin seeds and popcorn in front of our local cinema. In those days we didn't have all those flavoured snacks, crisps and other chemical ingenuities, designed to attract the eye and ruin diet and health. Corn and pumpkins were in abundance. But so were pride and vanity. Most people would rather die than be seen with a basket in front of a cinema, selling seeds and popcorn! That guy didn't care. To him, that was his source of income and his livelihood. And what a source it was!

You too can become successful, extraordinary or rich by doing things others don't want to do or don't like doing. Success does not lie in certain areas or some glorified professions. It is everywhere. Just ask yourself one simple question: Would you rather be the owner of the best and most professional recycling business in town or a mediocre, ordinary lawyer in a local court? My choice is obvious. What is yours?

 STORY

Rosenbluth International Inc. is a company that owes its success to Hal Rosenbluth's contrarian management philosophy. Hal advocates that one's employees should come first and foremost, even before the customer. He believes in "perpetual training", afternoon tea sessions with his employees, regular "happiness barometer" meetings (which gauge employees' satisfaction) and upward evaluations, where supervisors and managers get evaluated.

Hal Rosenbluth is also a "salmon man". His office is decorated with dozens of salmon of all sizes and materials – a stuffed toy salmon, a chocolate salmon, a beanbag salmon. "The salmon swims upstream, against the tide, taking on obstacles others won't. That's us. We're contrarians. So we picked the salmon as our company mascot," says Rosenbluth.[14]

8

Getting To Know Yourself

Diagnose Your Situation Correctly

"Then you shall judge yourself," the king answered. "That is the most difficult thing of all. It is much more difficult to judge oneself than to judge others. If you succeed in judging yourself rightly, then you are indeed a man of true wisdom."
Antoine de Saint-Exupery, *The Little Prince*

Self-analysis is a check-up we perform on ourselves. To reach the right conclusions and to form a correct picture and opinion of yourself, you have to arrive at a correct diagnosis. To arrive at a correct diagnosis, you have to realise that diagnosis is a process of systematic, sequential elimination. You eliminate all things that you are not and arrive at those that you are. Most people start from the opposite end. They form a picture of what they think they are and use everything possible to justify their "findings". In doing that they certainly succeed in proving what they want to prove, but almost always what they want to prove is a wrong diagnosis of their condition and a distorted picture of their true "self".

RECIPE

Correct diagnosis is the first step to self-healing.

Many people will read this book: some will be curious and will want to know what KAIZEN is and how it relates to their lives; others will browse through it, looking for simple recipes so they can immediately apply them in their improvement efforts. Why are you reading this book? Is it because your life basically works and you want to achieve even more? Or is it because your life doesn't work the way you would like it to, so you need guidance in your striving for the solutions to your problems?

Recognise The Need To Improve

"So it is said that if you know others and know yourself, you will not be imperilled in a hundred battles; If you do not know others but you know yourself, you win one and you lose one; if you do not know others and do not know yourself, you will be imperilled in every single battle."

Sun Tzu, The Art of War

Most problems people have in their lives are created by themselves. Some are caused by wrong attitudes, some by unrealistic expectations, some by lack of purpose, persistence and knowledge. There are many more other reasons, some of which will be discussed throughout this book.

The old social contract, the one that governed lives and careers of past generations, is dead. "If you work hard and give your best, you'll be rewarded. We'll take care of you and the benefits of your work will follow." Although this contract was, of course, just implied, many individuals entrusted their well-being to the hands of their employers, who never signed on the dotted line – it was a contract with only one signatory. Loyalty was a one-way street anyway.

As individuals began to realise that many employers don't reward achievements fairly, that they cannot be trusted to take care of their future, the importance of taking one's destiny into one's own hands started to emerge. Not many people were or still are able to interpret the alarm signals correctly. Instead of accepting the reality with composure and confidence, they search for causes and falsely attribute them to other people, employers, themselves or external causes or events. Problems and causes are seldom located within oneself, more often with others. The crucial aspect of that blame-shift is the postponement. The longer we postpone accepting responsibility for our own development, the more painful and the more difficult the transition is going to be and the longer it will take to start achieving results in one's improvement programme.

 STORY

"Later, bringing a snack of fish and sake, she pointed out a dignified man who, though sitting up rigidly in his seat, seemed to be sleeping. He was, she said, a Noh actor from Kyoto, well-known for his playing of the part of a Chinese lion, especially on television.

Always, while flying, he sits in this position thinking how he might make his next performance more refined."[15]

Accept Responsibility For Your Own Development

"How do you expect us to fly as you fly?" came another voice.
"You are special and gifted and divine, above other birds."
"Look at Fletcher! Lovell! Charles-Roland! Are they also special and gifted and divine? No more than you are, no more than I am. The only difference, the very only one, is that they have begun to understand what they really are and have begun to practise it."
Richard Bach, Jonathan Livingston Seagull

When you accept responsibility for your own development, you will abandon old, non-productive concepts, stop playing futile psychological games you have been playing with yourself and others and start examining various paradigms you have lived with in the past. You will also feel motivated and obliged to start doing things that have to be done, not just those you feel like doing, those you habitually have been doing or those that seems most reasonable or appropriate to do.

Gautama Siddhartha, better know as Buddha (the enlightened one), emphasises in his teachings that the betterment of society depends on the betterment of the individual, while political philosophies such as Marxism propagate a point of view that society has to be dealt with and put right first, and the individual's improvement will follow. The first view is inductive in nature (from a single entity to the whole), the later deductive (from the whole to the individual).

Which view would you subscribe to?

Define Your Own Philosophy In Life

"There are many paths to the top of the mountain, but the view is always the same."

Chinese proverb

Sooner or later, every human being has to die. Mentally, try to put yourself in that perspective. Imagine your time on Earth is coming to an end and you have to part ways with your loved ones, your friends, family and everybody else you got to know over the years. Think about your epitaph. What do you think people would engrave on your tombstone? How would they remember you? What mark would you leave imprinted in the life you left behind?

Then ask yourself: How would I like people to remember me? What would I like my epitaph to be? What regrets would I have? What unfulfilled dreams would I take with me?

It is always difficult to compare our own opinion of ourselves with those of others. We often judge ourselves by our successes, while others judge us by our failures. Or we often evaluate our performance on the basis of what we are capable of doing, while others evaluate what we actually do.

If you succeed in defining the difference between your final judgement of yourself with that of others, you'll have a much better idea of what you have to do to close that gap and eliminate the difference.

Develop Your Mission Statement And Live It

Every organisation and individual with a mission in life, be it in private life or career, should have a mission statement. A mission statement is the essence of all your efforts, knowledge, plans and goals. It should clearly, simply and explicitly state what you are trying to achieve. This was, for example, my mission statement in writing this book:

To help people in their self-actualisation efforts by providing inspirational, unbiased, systematic, no-nonsense, inexpensive advice on major self-awareness and self-improvement issues.

 EXERCISE

What is your mission statement? Write it in the space below and look at it every morning when you wake up and every night before you go to bed.
My mission statement is:

✍...

....

....

Your mission statement is not a mere sentence on a piece of paper. It has to be a living document. It must become a part of your life; in other words, you have to live your mission statement. Your thoughts, actions and plans have to be consistent with your mission statement. Lack of consistency or commitment to following your mission is a death sentence to your constant improvement efforts. Only by applying your philosophy to life will you become the person you want to become. As soon as you start living someone else's philosophy and following someone else's cause, you become someone else, not the person you wanted to become.

Audit Your Personal Mission Statement Regularly

Equally dangerous would be to blindly accept your mission statement and rigidly adhere to it. Your mission has to be flexible and adaptable. It isn't cast in stone, because its purpose is to deal creatively with the issues and problems of both today and tomorrow.

The mission statement is just a guiding light. Its purpose is to guide you in your daily living and to serve as a framework for your continuous improvement. It won't provide the details on how to behave in various situations, what course of action to take or what to say. It will, however, make it easier for you to do all those things.

Over time, inconsistencies between what we really do and what we proclaim we should be doing tend to grow and diverge. Regular audits of your mission statement and examination of those inconsistencies will reveal how far you are from where you want to be. The quality of the questions you ask yourself will determine the quality of your results:

- What are my alternatives?
- What are the pros and cons of each alternative?
- What developments could affect my mission?
- What knowledge and skills will I need to complete my mission successfully?
- Where and how do I acquire the knowledge and develop the skills needed?
- How will my choices affect my future?
- What are the critical factors of my success?
- How do I control and achieve those critical factors?

While your mission statement clarifies your main hopes, aims and objectives into a single, concise message, a vision statement helps you to identify, understand and focus on what you want to achieve and to develop the strategies and tactics to get there. Vision aligns you with your purpose and makes it easier to learn how certain efforts you make contribute towards your eventual success. Enhance you mission statement with a vision statement.

Your highest vision, the cord that resonates with the greatest strength and vigour, should become your mission statement, your greatest passion. When you reflect on your visions, discuss them with others, analyse them, constantly recreate and refine them as you progress in your self-actualisation efforts, they shift from a mere notion towards becoming a reality.

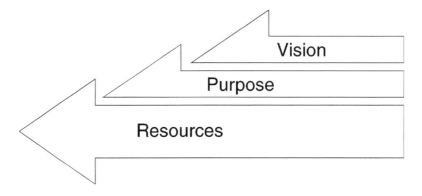

Figure 13. Alignment of vision, purpose and resources

Set Some Time Aside For Quiet Thoughts

"One ought, every day at least, to hear a little song, read a good poem, see a fine picture, and, if it were possible, to speak a few reasonable words."
Goethe, *Wilhelm Meister's Apprenticeship, V, 1*

STORY

Sidney Rittenberg spent sixteen years in a Chinese prison, most of it in solitary confinement. The first question asked after he returned to the United States was how he managed to stay sane during all those years of solitude. He answered: "Every day I tried to set some time aside to think quietly about life."

The moral: If a prisoner confined to his solitary cell needed some time to analyse life and think about it, don't you think you also need some time to think about your life and career? Have you set some time aside and devoted it to yourself? How much time have you set aside? Are you getting to know yourself better?

Reflection is a tool known only to humans. Animals rely primarily on instincts and genetic responses inherited from their ancestors. In that sense, reflection is a unique human quality, the one that directly leads and naturally lends itself to learning and improvement.

The primary inducement for reflecting on our experiences is failure and difficulties. When everything seems to be fine and we are going along quite well, we seldom take the time to reflect on our successfulness, but this is precisely the time when we should make the effort of analysing our positive experiences and achievements. Somehow it seems that we are more influenced and shaped by our negative experiences, so we have to make a habit of reflecting on positives too, not just on the negatives.

Reprogramme Your Self-Instructions

Unconscious decisions and self-instructions of various kinds and origins burden our lives with confusing conflicts, mixed feelings, unfinished psychological transactions and incomplete relationships.

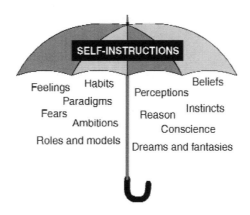

Figure 14. Sources of self-instructions.

9

Framing And Reframing Your Mind

Review Your Self-Concept

"Well, what are you? What is it about you that you have always known as yourself? What are you conscious of in yourself: your kidneys, your liver, your blood vessels? No. However far back you go in your memory it is always some external manifestation of yourself where you come across your identity: in the work of your hands, in your family, in other people. And now, listen carefully. You in others – this is what you are, this is what your consciousness has breathed, and lived on, and enjoyed throughout your life, your soul, your immortality – your life in others."

Boris Pasternak, *Doctor Zhivago*

Continuous improvement is a process of growth in all spheres of private and corporate life. The Western concept of "self" normally tends to separate the individual's identities and draws arbitrary lines between oneself and others. The struggle of achievement is the struggle based on finding one's own way, developing one's own identity and then trying to maintain that identity by distinguishing oneself from others. Working life is separate from private life and in different situations different aspects of one's personality and identity are prominent.

KAIZEN breaks barriers between those separate categories and

113

establishes concentric circles of relationships. It is from those relationships that one's identity is derived. All influences, synergy, collaborationism, beliefs and experiences flow within those circles of relationships. To try to "find oneself" by detachment and separation from others would be a counterproductive and futile exercise. One's identity is partially derived from those within one's inner circles of relationships. Interdependence is a key relational concept within our circles of relationships, the mooring line that establishes ties with the family, friends, co-workers, management.

Don't search for success only within yourself – turn outward. The easiest way to become successful is to let others make you successful. The odds of achieving success all by yourself are very, very remote. Success is around you, but you have to recognise it and be on the lookout all the time.

QUESTION

How do others respond to you? What makes them act and behave the way they do towards you?

Have Confidence And Belief In Small Improvements

"Drugs are not always necessary. Belief in recovery always is."
Norman Cousins, *Anatomy of an Illness*

Creative expectancy is a psychological underlay of the magic carpet that flies towards self-improvement. If, when you desire something, you devise ways of achieving it, plan your actions towards that goal and *strongly believe in the positive outcome of your efforts*, this will go a long way to achieving the desired result. Believing in small improvements is easier than believing in breakthroughs and quantum leaps, and belief is the first step towards self-confidence and confidence in the system of continuous improvement.

Those who succeed through continuous improvement believe that they can make a difference in their own lives and in the lives of others.

They believe that as much as the world has an impact on them, they can have a significant impact on their environment too. Champions are determined to instigate as much positive change as possible, to touch the lives of others and make them better.

EXERCISE

Think of three things you could change (improve, rectify, repair, introduce, establish, ...) right now, no matter how small or insignificant those issues may be. Then, go out and do it!

These are the three small improvements I will make right now:

✍ ....

....

....

....

....

....

....

Systems-thinking recognises the fact that many obvious solutions ultimately don't work. They may produce some results and improvements on a short-term scale, but could even make things worse in the long run. In his book *The Fifth Discipline*, Peter Senge claims that:

"Small, well-focused actions can sometimes produce significant, enduring improvements, if they're in the right place. Systems thinkers refer to this principle as 'leverage.' Tackling a difficult problem is often a matter of seeing where the high leverage lies, a change which-with a minimum of effort-would lead to lasting, significant improvement."[16]

FURTHER READING: *The Fifth Discipline*

The Fifth Discipline is a book about "learning organisations". The key to managing change and improvement in an organisation is the ability to use the commitment of individuals and their capacity to learn at all levels. The author, Peter Senge, identifies five crucial factors for the success of the learning organisation: systems thinking, personal mastery, mental modes, shared vision and team learning.(Peter M. Senge, Random House Australia, 1992)

Separate Reality From Perception

"All our knowledge has its origins in our perceptions."
Leonardo da Vinci

The concept of reality in terms of which we perceive our lives plays a crucial role in our self-actualisation and self-improvement efforts. The better we perceive our realities and their dimensional multiplicity, the easier it will be to harness the powers of the environment and those of others for the mutual benefit.

By relating to it in the plural, I hinted at the fact that individual realities differ from person to person. Each individual has some unique characteristics, possesses some outstanding skills or knowledge, plans some individual goals, fights some internal battles. The reality of the surrounding world, however, is pretty much the same for large groups of people that share the same way of living. The life of Eskimos hasn't got much in common with the life of an American executive, but we can say with great certainty that most American executives do share a very similar reality.

REFLECTION

The environmental reality is the same for all of us; what varies are our individual perceptions of that reality.

One of the preconditions for continuous improvement is a gradual expanded perception of one's reality which goes beyond your present boundaries and paradigms. Furthermore, what is needed is a separation of reality from your perception of that reality, which may give a distorted and inaccurate picture and hinder your planning, orientation and positioning in life.

Differentiate Between Money And Wealth

Working for money is only a start towards creating material wealth. The crucial step is saving a percentage of that money. That is your capital, the seed that will eventually turn into a harvest. Those grains have to be invested into a scheme of some kind, which will multiply the amount saved and compound itself many times over. This effectively means that any surplus funds created have to be left in the scheme to enable it to bear fruit. That is the harvest time.

RECIPE

Wealth should not be one's aim; it is the process of creating wealth and pursuing goals that enlivens life, not the wealth itself.

To be or to have? The collectors play "Whoever dies with the most possessions wins." The improvers' game is called "Let's see, can I get over that obstacle and enjoy myself in the process?". The message is: renounce the collector's mentality!

QUESTION

When faced with a proposal or an opportunity, what is usually the first question that comes to your mind?

- *What's in it for me?*
- *What can I learn from this?*
- *How could this help me in reaching my goals?*
- *How can I use my skills and talents best to help the cause?*

Reconcile Paradoxes

"The paradoxes of today are the prejudices of tomorrow, since the most benighted and the most deplorable prejudices have had their moment of novelty when fashion lent them its fragile grace."
Marcel Proust, *Pleasures and Regrets*

A paradox is a concept, situation or a statement that appears to be a contradiction and impossibility, but is often true and possible. To understand a paradox one has to understand all the conditions attached to it and the context in which the paradox is analysed. What at first seemed contradictory, unfeasible, improbable or illogical, after careful consideration will reveal itself as quite a plausible and normal situation.

Paradox does not just confuse issues and make them appear absurd or fallacious, it can also serve as an attention grabber; its sometimes shocking impossibility underscores and emphasises the often profound truth behind it.

PARADOX

Expect nothing; be prepared for anything.Samurai saying

Respond Rather Than React

"Every tomorrow has two handles: We can take hold of it with the handle of anxiety and uncertainty or the handle of faith and confidence."

Henry Ward Beecher

There are two levels of acting when a person is subjected to outside developments, stimuli and the actions of others. The first level is reacting. Reacting is intuitive, archaic, instinctive response coded in our genes. It is our tool for psychological self-defence, provided by nature as "standard equipment." It takes no special skill or knowledge to react in some way; everyone is capable of reacting.

Responding, the second level, is based on the restraint of one's reactions and on the ability to withhold those rapid and instinctive reactions and substitute them with controlled, logical and more rational responses.

DEFINITION

Events + responses = outcomes

Responding is a conscious, controlled action which channels your energy into the attainment of the benefits and results you aim for. Reacting is the one and only principal behaviour when confronted with the demands of life and other people. Responding comprises a much larger and wider repertoire of behaviours, which we consciously choose either to minimise the negative impact our environment may have on us, or to maximise its positive impact.

Louis Thurstone, a psychological tester, believed in the ability to control rapid, instinctive reactions and to substitute them with more rational and systematic responses.[17] Although intuition, feelings and emotions have their own important place in the art of continuous improvement, instinctive response to problems is seldom the best way of finding solutions.

Recognise The Shades Of Grey

"I know that you, ladies and gentlemen, have a philosophy, each and all of you, and that the most interesting and important thing about you is the way in which it determines the perspective in your several worlds."

William James

KAIZEN is not absolute; it's relative and situational. While the Western colour palette ultimately rests on two opposites, black and white, constant improvement recognises shades of grey. There is no such duality. What may seem like a negative experience or adversity (losing a job, death of a loved one, business failure, etc.) is not a completely negative experience. In every adversity, there is always a hidden element of opportunity to learn, improve, think and benefit.

ACTION
Eliminate the concept of good and bad from your thinking.Learn to recognise the shades of grey.

Start Pretending And Imitating

The power of autosuggestion is enormous. Acting or pretending can be an extremely useful concept for breaking barriers, either real or imagined. Regardless of the fact that you are not able to do something properly or that you haven't mastered all aspects of a task or craft, if you act as if you are able, as if you have mastered it, you will align your inner beliefs with your ultimate aim. You will gradually convince your subconscious mind that the reality you are faking is in fact real, that you are able to do what you set to do, and that you are in control of events you couldn't control before.

DEFINITION

Pretending is the next best thing to being.

Imitation is another powerful tool in the growth tool kit. It is the main tool in our early development, the one children and young adults use widely and naturally, until it gets suppressed at a later stage, to be used infrequently, only as a result of conscious effort. It is illustrative that *manabu*, Japanese word for learning, originates from *manebu*, which means "to imitate."

Know Your Values And Premises

"Life is the art of drawing sufficient conclusions from insufficient premises."

Samuel Butler

How do we go about defining our values? Soul searching; thinking about what different things mean to you and how different things, people, actions and concepts make you feel or behave; feeling your inner beliefs and analysing them; analysing your premises and conceptions.

Premises are assumptions we normally don't evaluate, those we take for granted and use as our starting points and origins of our thoughts and beliefs. Premises shape our values and surface in the way we behave, talk, act and think. Many of your own premises are hard to evaluate. The good news is that by examining and analysing some, you could improve your understanding of the rest.

DEFINITION

Self-improvement is nothing but a continuous act of defining, refining and living your values.

121

Values are relatively vague notions. You can clarify the concept of values by reminding yourself on a regular basis to think about the forces that shape your actions and your whole approach to life. To clarify your values, write them down. Some will be easy to express explicitly; some will have to be left in an implicit form, at least until you crystallise your thinking and refine them into a cohesive, potent statement.

The best indicator of your values is the way you spend your resources. The more resources you spend on or commit to something, the more you value it. By analysing the way you spend your most important resources (such as time and money), you can get a quite accurate indication of your guiding values.

The ability to reflect on your values, to organise them into a cohesive and congruent system, to commit yourself to them and to periodically assess their appropriateness, means to have an organised and focused approach to your life. Choosing your values means choosing a quality of life based on those values. Living your values means voluntarily and consciously opting for the behaviour that is guided by those values and framed by them.

STRATEGY

Articulate your values; reduce the conflict between your values and your behaviour. When you align your actions with your values, your performance is certain to improve.

Winning is not a couple of big wins, with periods of inactivity in between. Winning is a never-ending succession of small wins, through which an unstoppable momentum and a winning tradition is created. So come and join the KAIZEN cause. You have nothing to lose but your old premises and preconceived notions, while you can gain new insights and ways of seeing.

Install Effective Shock Absorbers

When trouble comes, it has to be dealt with. When the ride gets rough, there are two options in front of you. You can simply turn back and start heading in the opposite direction and then try to find a different road that will lead you to the same destination, or you can equip yourself with shock absorbers to make your ride more pleasant. Rough patches are more of an exception than a rule and usually don't last very long. In most cases, consider staying on your current path.

DEFINITION

Growing smarter means growing stronger. Accumulating knowledge, skills and know-how is more important than accumulating power, prestige and tangible assets.

When accidents happen (and they do happen quite often), capitalise on them. Take advantage of them. Find the seed of opportunity in every adversity. Bounce back as quickly as you can. Use the power and the momentum of your fall to bounce back as high as possible, and in the process of bouncing back don't forget the most important thing – don't take yourself too seriously. Learn to laugh in the difficult times. Say to yourself: "I've never let those little things get me down."

Effective shock absorbers let you spring back into action as soon as you hit the floor. They will always remind you not to expect perfection either from yourself or from others (especially not from others) and help you see yourself in lighter way.

Read Winnie-the-Pooh

"That buzzing-noise means something. You don't get a buzzing-noise like that, just buzzing and buzzing, without its meaning something. If there's a buzzing-noise, somebody's making a buzzing-noise, and the only reason for making a buzzing-noise that I know of is because you're a bee."

Then he thought another long time and said: "And the only reason for being a bee that I know of is making honey."
And then he got up, and said: "And the only reason for making honey is so I can eat it." So he began to climb the tree.
A. A. Milne, *Winnie-the-Pooh*

A. A. Milne's *Winnie-the-Pooh* is a children's storybook character. Winnie and his friends live in a forest, which provides its never-ending challenges to little Winnie and his companions, the Owl, the Donkey and the Rabbit. Milne's characterisation is well worth attention, simply because it portrays various human personalities or even different aspects of one's own psyche.

Eeyore the Donkey, often distressed and irritated, constantly complains, but never takes any action towards the resolution of his problems and upsets. The Owl, symbolising wisdom and prudence, shows off his wisdom through his pompous demeanours and self-proclaimed statesmanship, but that wisdom rarely finds solutions to problems. The Rabbit, an impulsive hustler, calculates and analyses, but never grasps the reality, unable to break the barrier of practicality.

Winnie, however, accepts the inevitable, keeps an eye on what's important and stays calm and composed. He realises that his chances of success are the greatest by being patient, staying calm and doing all he can in a given situation. Although Winnie patiently accepts the inevitable and faces the reality, he keep his mind firmly focused on the "honey".

In his book *The Tao of Pooh*, Benjamin Hoff draws parallels between Winnie-the-Pooh and the Taoist philosophy of acceptance and prevention of interference of unproductive mental barriers. "Within each of us there is an Owl, a Rabbit, an Eeyore, and a Pooh," Hoff concludes. "For too long we have chosen the way of Owl and Rabbit. Now, like Eeyore, we complain about the results. But that accomplishes nothing. If we are smart, we will choose the way of Pooh. As if from far away, it calls to us with the voice of a child's mind. It may be hard to hear at times, but it is important just the same, because without it we will never find our way through the forest."[18]

10

Motivating Yourself And Fuelling Your Excellence

Find Out What Motivation Means To You

"Disappointment, when it involves neither shame nor loss, is as good as success; for it supplies as many images to the mind, and as many topics to the tongue."

Samuel Johnson

Motivating an individual is a daunting task. External motivation has been proven to be only a very short-term solution, which in turn becomes ineffective and cannot sustain success. Internal, motivation, the one that comes within and stays there, is the fuel of excellence. The best way to trigger that inner drive and awaken the spirit of achievement is by making people think for themselves. This is probably the best description of this book's aim – to help you start thinking for yourself, to be critical about opinions, methods and advice others may try to impose on you and to be more confident in your own ideas, dreams and perceptions.

DEFINITION

Motivation is simply an inner drive for success, a mental force that induces action and helps overcoming setbacks.

There are two basic groups of motivating agents: avoiding the negative and pursuing the positive. Avoiding the negative means preventing loss of something or someone (loss of income, loss of a loved person, decline of health, loss of life, loss of face, reputation, or social standing or status, etc.), avoiding pain and hardship, and preserving one's life and lifestyle. The pursuit of positive is the pursuit of something we perceive as desirable (knowledge, beauty, money, material possessions, fame, pleasure, power, longevity, etc.). Some psychologists are of the opinion that motivators which are based on avoiding the negative are more powerful than those that motivate by seeking and gaining the positive.

EXERCISE

Think about your sources of motivation. What makes your world spin around? List your positive motivators below. Whenever you find yourself down and out, think about your motivators and let them do their job. Let them motivate you.

Specific persons, things or ideas that provide my motivation:

✍ ....

....

....

....

....

....

....

Motivation and inspiration are two closely related terms that are often interchanged and used in the same context, but they have slightly different meanings. The difference in being "motivated" and being "inspired" is primarily in the time frame and permanency of the stimulation. Motivation is considered more permanent and longer-term state of mind than inspiration, which is a state of enlightenment and desire which often leads to action of some kind, but which usually lacks the permanency and fails to sustain the motivational level. Motivation coupled with inspiration is a powerful force that can sustain the commitment to continuous improvement despite doubts, setbacks and various forms of hardship.

Harness The Power Of Inspirational Dissatisfaction

"Most ordinary people lived their lives in boxes, as bees did in cells."

Theodore H. White

The best recipe for motivation for change is to discover your own sources of dissatisfaction and discontent with your present and to articulate them through your goals and aims. This could be achieved either by comparing where you are with where you want to be (building your own vision of your future) or by being constantly on a lookout for small discrepancies, inadequacies and imperfections, all of which are opportunities for incremental, focused improvements.

Boredom is one of the biggest inspirational dissatisfaction motivators. Many high achievers would do anything to escape that sinking feeling of being bored. People who are easily bored constantly strive for better jobs, more cooperative co-workers, better performance, new challenges and responsibilities. They are the champions, the self-improvers. Boredom pushes those people into new adventures and towards higher achievements. If you are bored easily, count it as a blessing in disguise.

RECIPE

Be easily bored. Don't surrender to conformity and complacency. Be inspirationally dissatisfied with yourself, your environment and your goals and aspirations. Constantly strive to improve all three.

Link Your Motivation With Your Goals

Why is it important to link personal motivation and one's goals? Because for most people motivation is something sporadic, non-focused and scattered. It's something ill-defined, something latent and not well harnessed or expressed. Without goals and aims that can serve as an anchor, motivation isn't enough to prevent us from drifting aimlessly in the sea of life. Only when one's motivation is applied and focused on well defined, worthwhile goals does it become a potent force that eliminates obstacles and facilitates achievement.

Doing old things and routine tasks slightly better and repeating the ordinary pattern of your daily activities, no matter how successful they may be, needs to be accentuated with new stimuli. New ways of doing old tasks, new people, new environments provide a shifting viewpoint, a contrast to the established patterns and mostly ordinary activities.

Reward yourself with such contrasts. Differentiate and contrast what is and has been with what can or could be. Stimulate yourself with novelty. Try options and explore viewpoints. When you decentre, you evolve from an individual view to a view which recognises and considers other perspectives.

Before you take any action, think about possible outcomes and positive results that are associated with those outcomes. Help your mind by simplifying your thoughts and single out the benefit that appeals to you the most, and make that benefit your motivational beacon to guide you through the course of your chosen action. Make it your main motivator in that instance by associating benefits with your actions.

For each action, select your prime motivator, create a vivid mental picture of it and study it every now and then.

Set Up Your Own Reward System

Don't forget to reward yourself for every success, no matter how small, every goal achieved, every milestone reached. If you don't provide your own rewards, you will seek those rewards from others and become a victim of dependency on others' opinions and approval of your actions. By producing your own rewards and motivation you'll shift from being outer-dependent to being inner-dependent. Instead of being directed and rewarded by others you'll be directed and rewarded by yourself.

To reward yourself means to motivate yourself, and motivation is closely linked with your own feeling of self-worth. Your feeling of self-worth and your own standards of thinking and behaviour are the basis of your self-rewarding system and the starting point in relinquishing your dependence on external approval.

The reward system our employers, educators and society as a whole uses is shameful. In many cases it's completely absent; yes, that's right – it doesn't exist. The system overcompensates underachievers and undercompensates high achievers. In corporations and institutions where some sort of system does exist, it's rarely used, and when it's used, it's geared to the short term, simply because everything else is geared to the short term. Your aim is a long-term commitment to improvement, which cannot depend on a short-term motivation and reward.

 REFLECTION

Some shrewd owners of self-service restaurants and coffee shops have discovered that desserts sell better when placed at the start of the line instead of at the end, where they 'normally' and 'logically' seem to belong. In one of them there is a sign that explains it all: "Eat dessert first; life is so short."

Take Criticism As Feedback On Your Performance, Not Your Personality

By providing your own motivational and reward system you will be true to yourself. It will help you bridge the gap between what you are currently and what you are striving to become. Your own reward system will put you in control of your own destiny and make you free to exercise that self-control.

Other people can be dangerous. Most of them don't care about your self-actualisation and self-improvement efforts. Why should you then allow their indifference, jealousy or ridicule to limit you or control you in any way? Why should you base your feeling of self-worth on the opinions of others? Don't take the opinions of others as a determinant of your value, but only as an indicator how others perceive you. Be secure in your sense of self.

Others identify you through your actions and equate their perception of your worthiness with the manifestations of your actions. It would be self-defeating to accept such perception of yourself as your own. Your intrinsic value cannot be the same as the value of your actions. A feeling of inadequacy, guilt and low self-esteem is a direct consequence of our perceptions that we haven't met the standards others have imposed on us.

KAIZEN distinguishes between your own intrinsic worth and your extrinsic value, which is perceived and developed by others, and which may fluctuate. Criticism should not be taken personally, as an attack on your innate value as a person, but simply as a feedback on your work, ideas or actions.

Keep Recharging Your Batteries

Constant improvement does not simply mean improving what you've currently got. It means much more – acquiring new skills and knowledge, developing various aspects of your personality and integrating them into your own system of values, productive habits, relationships and thought patterns. It also means abandoning unproductive concepts, ideas and efforts, preventing activities which are not valuable investments of your feelings, knowledge, time, money and other assets.

The concept of KAIZEN is based on the principle of self-renewal. Like the mythological bird Phoenix, with its ability to rise from its own ashes, a self-improver constantly refreshes himself through periods of rest and reflection, which recharge his batteries and provide him with new energy and enthusiasm.

 STORY

One Christmas I got a teddy bear that played the drums," says Dan Clark, a motivational speaker in Salt Lake City. "I thought it was great as I opened the box. Then I noticed the reminder, 'Batteries required.'

For three days, the bear sat on a shelf with its mouth open and its arms in the air. And I realized: That's how many of us spend our lives. We're ready for action, but don't have the batteries."[19]

11

Cutting The Strings That Pull You Back

Recognise Your Paradigms

As we walk through the alley of life, we collect stories, clichés and experiences and build our lives on them. They serve as a memory bank and a reference library that stores data, principles and situations which help us handle various situations by comparing them to past references and drawing up comparisons and conclusions.

Paradigm means an example or model and usually relates to an accepted, habitual or mandatory ways of doing, seeing, thinking or comprehending. Paradigms establish boundaries for such a process and prescribe norms of acceptable or successful behaviour within those limits.

A shift in paradigms is the first step towards change. To achieve such a shift, you have to recognise and accept your paradigms, as well as to recognise their nature and the changes they have been going through. The ever-changing nature of some of our paradigms makes them prime candidates to KAIZEN-style improvement. Others are more defined, more permanent and therefore more difficult to change.

Any new thought, idea or unfamiliar concept or theory has to survive the scrutiny of our mind sets based on their paradigms and preconceived notions which are in most cases firmly embedded in our psyche. This is why changing our ways of thinking and behaving is so far from easy. Changing one's own paradigms and a whole mind set is the most difficult aspect of self-improvement. It is also the most rewarding aspect, because the road towards success and fulfilment starts in the mind.

ACTION

Become a paradigm shifter. Spot the new and emerging paradigms and capitalise on them. Fight the old and stale ones when they start impeding your progress.

Make A Habit Out Of Habit-breaking

"One might call habit a moral friction: something that prevents the mind from gliding over things but connects it with them and makes it hard for it to free itself from them."

G. C. Lichtenberg

Although KAIZEN itself is not about departing significantly from the way things have been done and the way problems have been solved in the past, leaving the routines of your life and departing from your normal way of thinking could be beneficial. Pushing out your perimeter fences or, better still, tearing them down, is the way to begin seeing world from a different perspective, from a shifted standpoint, which usually brings new insights and enlightenment and changes the scripts you may be living by.

Scripts that people live are numerous, but very similar:

• I want to be able to choose, but I want someone else to decide for me.
• I want to be left alone; I don't want too much excitement.
• I'm afraid I'll repeat my mistakes.
• Nobody seems to understand me.
• I hate myself and I hate others.
• I cannot find my purpose in life.

- Whatever I touch goes wrong; I cannot do anything properly.
- I don't want to start anything; what's the point, it won't end up well, anyway.
- My life is a continuous sequence of failures and losses.
- Nothing nice ever happens to me, just failures and disappointments.

ACTION

Challenge your old views and analyse your usual patterns. Make a conscious decision and commitment to embrace other views and paradigms.

Unload Burdens From Your Past

When you set your goals, you should also devote time to thinking about obstacles that may stand in your way towards achieving them. This shouldn't be too difficult; most people are good at finding obstacles, excuses and the reasons why things won't work as they've planned. You'll do it differently. Instead of using those obstacles, difficulties and hurdles as excuses for not following up on your goals and for giving up on them, you'll use them to think about the ways to eliminate them or to work out ways around them.

When you hit an obstacle (it isn't a matter of "if", but a certainty of "when") or make a mistake, don't equate that mistake with personal failure. Turn back, analyse what went wrong, when, how and why.

Then, for encouragement, survey your previous steps and think about your past successes. If you haven't already got one, make a list of your achievements in the past year or in the past three or five years and praise yourself for those achievements. Give yourself credit for a job well done and make yourself feel better about who you are and what you've done so far. Then, encouraged, go back to your temporary setback and attack it fiercely and wholeheartedly.

STORY

There is a story of an old man and a young boy who lived in ancient times. The old man was named Sartebus, and the boy was named Kim. Kim was an orphan, living on his own, making his way from village to village in search of food and a roof over his head. But most important of all, even more than his search for a full stomach and a comfortable, dry place to sleep, Kim was looking for something else – he was searching for **reason.** *"Why," he wondered, "do we travel throughout our lives in search of something we cannot find? Why must things be as difficult as they are? Do we make them so ourselves, or is it meant to be that we should struggle as we do?.*

These were wise thoughts for a boy as young as Kim, but it was just that kind of thinking that caused him to find along the way an old man, travelling the same road, who, Kim thought, might help him with an answer or two.

The old man was carrying on his back a large, covered, woven basket that appeared to be very heavy, especially for someone as old and weary as he was. When they stopped to rest beside a small brook along the road, the old man wearily settled his basket to the ground. To Kim it looked as though the man carried all of his worldly goods in that one basket; it seemed to be much heavier than even a much younger, stronger man could carry very far.

"What is in your basket that makes it so heavy?" Kim asked Sartebus. "I would be happy to carry it for you. After all, I am young and strong, and you are tired."

"It is nothing you could carry for me," answered the old man. "This is something I must carry for myself." And he added, "One day, you will walk your own road and carry a basket as weighted as mine."

Over many days and many roads, Kim and the old man walked many miles together. And although Kim often asked old Sartebus questions about why men must toil as they do, Kim did not learn from him any of the answers, nor could he learn, try as he might, what treasure of such great weight was in the basket the old man carried.

Sometimes late at night, at the end of a long day's journey, Kim would lie quietly, pretending to sleep, listening to the old man sorting through the contents of his basket by the flickering light from a small fire, and talking quietly to himself. But in the morning, as always, he would say nothing.

It was only when Sartebus could walk no more, and he lay down to rest for the last time, that he told young Kim his secret. In their last few hours together, he gave Kim not only the answer to the riddle of the basket he carried, but the answer to why men toil as they do.

"In this basket," Sartebus said, "are all of the things I believed about myself which were not true. They are the stones that weighed down my journey. On my back I have carried the weight of every pebble of doubt, every grain of the sand of uncertainty, and every millstone of misdirection I have collected along my way. Without these I could have gone so far. I could have lived a life of the dreams I saw in my mind. But with them I have ended up here, at the end of my journey." And without even unwrapping the braided cords that bound the basket to him, the old man closed his eyes and quietly went to sleep for the last time.

Before Kim himself went to sleep that night, he untied each cord that bound the basket to the old man and, lifting it free, carefully set it on the ground. When he had done this, he just as carefully untied the leather straps that held the woven cover in place, and lifted it aside. Perhaps because he had been looking for an answer to his own question, he was not at all surprised at what he found inside. The basket, which had weighed old man Sartebus down so long, was empty.

As we move from one experience to another, from one stage of life to the next, we face conflicts, doubts, insecurity, dilemmas, trials, adversity. Many of those conflicts, dilemmas and doubts are left unresolved and get carried away from one stage to another. To continue our development those burdens from the past have to be shed, conflicts resolved, doubts eliminated.

 FURTHER READING: *Life Cycle Completed*

Psychoanalyst Erik Erikson argues that life can be divided into eight stages, each with its dominant conflict which has to be resolved in order to proceed into the next stage. For him, our development is a succession of resolved conflicts. Infancy – basic trust vs. basic mistrust; Early childhood – autonomy vs. shame and doubt; Play age – initiative vs. guilt; School age – industry vs. inferiority; Adolescence – identity vs. identity confusion; Young adulthood – intimacy vs. isolation; Adulthood – generativity vs. stagnation; Old age – integrity vs. despair.(Erik Erikson, Norton, 1982)

Conquer Fear

"Until you are committed, there is hesitancy, the chance to draw back. Always ineffectiveness. With all acts of initiative and creation, there is one elementary truth, the ignorance of which kills countless ideas and splendid plans – the moment you definitely commit yourself, providence moves too.

"All sorts of things occur to help you that would never have occurred otherwise. A whole stream of events issues from the decision, raising in your favour all manner unforeseen incidents and meetings and material assistance, which no man could have dreamed would come his way.

"Whatever you can do, or dream you can, begin it. Boldness has genius, power and magic in it. Begin it now. "

Johann Wolfgang von Goethe

The rule for people who are not ambitious enough: make your appetites for success bigger than your fears. If your fears are holding you back and neutralising ambitions you may have, you have to eliminate the fears. Fears are the main cause of psychological slavery. By conquering them you become a master of your own destiny instead of a mere walking failure.

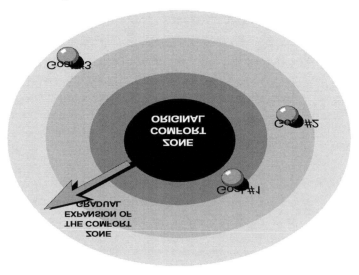

Figure 15. Expanding your comfort zone through the gradual attainment of ambitious goals.

Eliminate Psychological Slavery

People generally expect too much of their actions. They want actions that are not only approved by themselves, but ones that others approve as well. This expectation is the root cause of all failure in life.

Psychological dependence on others is a form of slavery, probably the most common form of psychological dependence of all. Its roots are in the early childhood. Unable to form accurate images of themselves, children rely on others to form those pictures for them. Their only guide is how others react to them. Due to their inability to critically analyse those assessments of others and question their authority and accuracy, they passively accept the judgements others pass on them. With most people, this habit is carried through their whole life. In his seminar "Self-Esteem And Peak Performance", Jack Canfield summarises that well when he says: "Some people would rather be right than successful."

Learn How To Deal With Crises

> *"Would you tell me," said Alice, a little timidly, "why you are painting those roses?" Five and Seven said nothing, but looked at Two. Two began in a low voice, "Why, the fact is, you see, Miss, this here ought to have been a red rose-tree, and we put a white one in by mistake; and if the Queen was to find it out, we should all have our heads cut off, you know."*
> Lewis Carroll, *Alice's Adventures in Wonderland*

In the Chinese and Japanese alphabet there is no single symbol for crisis. The ideogram for crisis is made up of two strokes of a pen. The first one stands for danger, the other for chance or opportunity. If translated literally, it means "Crisis is an opportunity riding the wind of danger". Whenever you face a difficulty, remember that seed of opportunity in any adversity and harness the power of that wind of danger!

Figure 16. Crisis = Danger + Opportunity.

A crisis is an unexpected development of events which may have unwanted consequences. Problems, crises and disputes are excellent opportunities to learn about ourselves, about the systems we operate within and about others. This valuable experience cannot be gained by reading books or attending courses. It is primarily a real life experience which should result in making less mistakes in the future.

Every negative, threatening, unpleasant or difficult situation is the opportunity to change individual and organisational prejudices, fallacies, biases, preconceived notions and outdated perceptions. Much-needed changes in the ways of working, thinking and operating can be accelerated, allowing fresh thinking and new views to emerge. Basically, every mistake made and every difficulty faced should be used to improve yourself professionally and personally.

Always turn every problem into opportunity, every disaster into a valuable experience. Opportunity often comes disguised as crises, misfortune or temporary defeat.

The unexpected does happen, crises do develop and trouble does emerge. When things start to go wrong, the course of events is usually uncertain. However, many unwanted problems can be anticipated or observed well in advance. Early warning signs should be recognised and taken seriously, not ignored. Instead of hoping that problems will somehow magically disappear, they have to be dealt with quickly, accurately and consistently.

Having an effective plan of action for dealing with crises can make all the difference between ultimate success or catastrophic failure. By definition, the contingency or crisis plan is only an outline of general principles, rules and guidelines. A detailed approach is impossible because of the very first descriptor of every problem or crises: unpredictability. Each particular situation will require a tailor-made plan, developed from the general contingency blueprint.

Give Up The Entitlement Ethic, Take Up A Cause

"We begin from the recognition that all beings cherish happiness and do not want suffering. It then becomes both morally wrong

140

and pragmatically unwise to pursue only one's own happiness oblivious to the feelings and aspirations of all others who surround us as members of the same human family. The wiser course is to think of others when pursuing our own happiness."
The Fourteenth Dalai Lama

We live in the Age of Entitlement. Generations ago, people found it normal to work hard and to make sacrifices not only for themselves and their families, but also for their countries and society as a whole. Today, the young don't want to work hard. They demand more from their employers, governments and society than they are willing to put in. They expect to be supported, encouraged and helped in their self-development and self- actualisation, in finding themselves, in their personal evolution; and on the other side they expect to be exempt from reciprocating and contributing something towards the well-being of society.

KAIZEN does not suit such selfish ways of thinking. It isn't merely a devotion to one's own goals and one's own cause, with no purpose and aims outside oneself and larger than oneself. The very nature of KAIZEN seeks a balance between "caring for oneself" and "caring for others", between individual and collective growth. It is impossible to single out yourself, as an individual, and improve while your environment stagnates. Entitlement does not exist in KAIZEN, only reciprocity.

Have you got a purpose beyond yourself? Have you got a cause you are devoted to? Having a purpose, something you are identifying yourself with and attached to, is necessary for achieving a breadth of vision and finding yourself.

Altruism is genuine interest in others and concern for their needs, interests and well-being. The question that should be asked is not "How can I get as much as possible from others and take from the world around me?" but "How can I, being who I am and where I am, make myself and others a little better, a little happier?"

141

RECIPE

Have a purpose outside yourself. Don't involve yourself exclusively with your own well being. Find a cause you feel strongly about and fight for it.

Leave A Legacy

"There is the true joy in life, the being used for a purpose recognised by yourself as a mighty one; the being thoroughly worn out before you are thrown on scrap heap; the being a force of Nature instead of a feverish selfish little clod of ailments and grievances complaining that the world will not devote itself to making you happy."

George Bernard Shaw

You and me, like every other human being, have a deeply instilled craving for significance. We want to be recognised, appreciated, valued. We aim to leave our mark on the lives of others, to achieve something valuable, something significant and universally accepted. Our deepest and most hidden latent goal is to leave a legacy.

Some of us write books and share their knowledge and experience with others who read our lines. You may be a painter, a sculptor or a poet, giving the world the pleasure of enjoyment of works of art. Our legacy is to share, to educate, to help.

Or you may be an engineer, a builder or a scientist, leaving behind you a monument, a bridge, an invention, a road that will bring the benefits of civilisation and technology to remote areas. Your legacy is to improve, to advance, to build.

Others save lives of those in trouble, those less fortunate, the sick and deprived, or they fight for human rights for animal rights, for the environment and the preservation of life on our planet. Their legacy is to preserve, to beautify, to prolong life.

Some people devote their entire lives to their families; they promote love and caring for others, for their children, neighbours and friends.

QUESTION

What have you done to improve, beautify or add value to the lives of others? What is the mark you are going to leave behind you? What is the legacy that will live on when you are not here any more?

12

Managing Your Individual Resources

Become A Steward Of Your Resources

Stewardship is the strategic use of one's potential and resources. The significance of stewardship in self-improvement is obvious – there is no point in improving your skills, raising your standards, carving your niche and positioning yourself, if those achievements, improvement and resources are not used efficiently and effectively. Stewardship is about allocating your resources such as time, energy and effort to activities that produce maximum return on that investment. Stewardship is also about making the right choices and selecting the options that work best and bring more rewards than others.

The Japanese expression *mottainai* literally means irreverent or impious, relating to the profanation of resources which are believed to be on only loan to us to manage and make the best use of. This kind of "sacred trust" is an important concept in Japanese philosophy, reflected in many other attitudes and teachings. The value concept of *mottainai* originates in ancient times and helps explain many attitudes towards work, natural resources and the way of life in Japan. Akio Morita, in his book *Made in Japan*, explains how such attitude developed:

"Struggling for survival under the constant threat of harsh times and natural calamity, attempting to produce goods with a minimum of raw materials, both became a way of life for the Japanese, and so the wasting of anything was considered shameful, virtually a crime. In the old days when Japan was completely isolated, we had to handle any calamity by means of our own resources. We had food shortages and earthquakes, and fires burned the wooden houses of our cities many times, forcing people to start rebuilding their lives from scratch. We became skilled at crisis management."[20]

Evaluate Probability

One of the concepts of KAIZEN that people have most trouble with is the concept of probability and choice. Since childhood days, humans are conditioned into dualism, into thinking that there are only two options, only two alternatives. Examining probabilities and evaluating options "in between" are not on the menu, and later in life many adults have difficulties in even understanding the concept, let alone using it effectively in daily choices.

Probability evaluation is about analysing options and estimating the consequences of alternative choices that could be made. It is about asking questions such as:

• What are my options at this moment and in this situation?
• What are the pros and cons of each option?
• What possible developments may have an impact on my options?
• How likely are those developments to happen?
• Which option is in line with my goals and my long-term strategy and aims?
• Which option is optimal from the viewpoint of speed, quality, effort and flexibility?
• Which option is the best value, the best return on investment?

Our optimism and positive expectations are inversely proportional with the perceived difficulty of the task in front of us. In other words, we overestimate our chances of success in carrying out tasks or solving problems that we perceive as easy ones and we underestimate our chances of being successful in performing tasks and carrying out assignments that seem difficult to us.

This obviously has a lot to do with probability estimating. We judge the probability of success in the case of easy assignments to be much higher than the probability for success at tackling jobs that appear more difficult or complex.

Build Your Foundations

"The heart of a lion cannot go far on the legs of a chicken."
Old Chinese saying

Every improvement in our lives has an understanding of human nature as its foundation. To advance and improve yourself, first you have to understand yourself. To improve your relationships with others, you'll have to get to know them a little better. An improvement has to be based on the existing foundations, just like every journey must have a starting point. The stronger you make your foundations, the more stable and stronger your advancement will be.

Compound Your Qualities and Assets

Compounding has been one of the key words in every successful man's vocabulary. Banks and other financial institutions own their existence and prosperity to it. So do wealthy individuals who were lucky or capable enough to compound their starting capital many times over. However, compounding doesn't necessarily apply exclusively to finance. It is an universal principle and can be applied to any field of human endeavour: knowledge, influence, skills, prestige, popularity, etc.

By compounding your qualities, the compounded qualities gradually, over time, always gain in value. Their value can never go down. It isn't what results and rewards you get in life, it isn't how you get it or how often. What makes a difference is what you do with what you get, how you invest, leverage and compound those achievements.

RECIPE

Use your money to create more money. Use your knowledge to gain new knowledge. Use your influence on people to become even more influential.

Become A Waste-Chaser

"Full many a gem of purest ray serene,
The dark unfathomed caves of ocean bear:
Full many a flower is born to blush unseen,
and waste its sweetness on the desert air."
Thomas Gray

Human resources are wasted on a scale still unknown to us, but certainly much greater than any other waste on earth. Some research has concluded that, on average, humans use only up to twenty per cent of their metal capacity. How correct this arbitrary figure is does not really matter. What matters is that by wasting ourselves, we are not as good, as happy or as successful as we could be.

The starting point in any self-improvement effort is to identify waste in one's life. Waste may take many forms and symptoms may vary. The immediate thought is always the waste of time, since time is our most precious resource. It cannot be replenished, stopped, reversed, speeded up or slowed down, or preserved for the future. It can only be used more or less efficiently.

Many other resources of an individual may be wasted. Health may be endangered through improper nutrition, lack of exercise, bad habits (smoking, consumption of alcohol) or lack of moderation in daily living. Financial resources may be wasted on assets, goods and services that lose their value (cars, holidays, luxury items) instead investing into income-producing assets that appreciate in value, such as real estate.

Waste is when resources are spent on activities and things that should not be done at all or should be done, but to a much lesser extent. Waste is also when opportunities are lost because resources are used for the wrong purposes. Measuring waste and the lost opportunities in particular is a difficult task in a life of an individual like you or me, but it isn't impossible. All it takes is to take things and actions you have taken at their face value and to analyse various alternatives you could have opted for instead.

Do Things Right The First Time

Give improvement a chance. Self-improvement is not possible until you recognise and admit to yourself that improvement is necessary. It always amazes me to see organisations, governments and individuals cut corners, rush jobs and put as little effort as possible into their projects and activities, only to be forced to have everything redone later, when it will take much more time, require much more effort and cost much more money than if it has been done properly in the first place.

 RECIPE

It is always cheaper, quicker and better to do things right the first time.Making errors is NOT inevitable and it is much cheaper to prevent errors than to deal with their consequences later.

Elevate Your Literacy Level

"There are techniques of being intelligent. It is not easy to acquire the proper use of the metal tools which we have thoughtlessly inherited or which are implicit in the construction of our brains. Severe effort and long practice are required."
Percy W. Bridgman

Literacy isn't only about the three Rs, "reading 'riting and 'rithmetic": it is about various abilities to observe and analyse the world around us and relate to it in a meaningful and productive manner. There are many possible ways to group and summarise literacy skills, so we'll arbitrarily adopt a functional approach, guided by the purpose of various literacy skills.

Professional literacy

When asked about what they do for a living, Westerners usually say something like "I'm an electrical engineer" or "I'm an accountant". Japanese, on the other hand, normally don't equate themselves with their profession, but with their company or their employer: "I work for Toyota" you will hear them say. While Westerners feel closer to defining themselves in terms of their occupation and professional skills, Japanese are more inclined to view themselves in sociological terms, where belonging and sharing are the most important concepts.

Professional literacy embraces both specialist and general knowledge one needs to perform duties of a certain profession or business.

Classical literacy

This is the essential form of literacy, what we usually call "the ability to read and write". It may seem hard to believe, but numerous studies have shown that a significant percentage of workers in the United Kingdom, America and Australia are "functionally illiterate". This basically means that they can read simple sentences in newspapers and magazines but are able to understand only the very simple concepts, topics and subjects to which they are accustomed (such as sport, sex and lottery information).

Cultural literacy

Cultural heritage, including values, customs, habits and norms prevalent in our environment (the workplace, educational system, judicial and governing system), should be understood and analysed. In your search for answers, in trying to understand why others behave or think the way they do, the answers can often be found in the cultural background, in the interaction between social structures and cultural paradigms.

Sociological literacy

To exist and function as individuals within a corporation and wider, as members of society, we have to understand the society we live in, its background, its norms, concepts, interactions and idiosyncrasies. We have to recognise the forces of interaction between groups, corporations, governments and individuals, and harness and promote the positive forces while fighting and resisting the negative ones.

Statistical literacy

History repeats itself in many ways and many times, over and over again. To learn from the experience of others, we compare situations and the factors that led to them. Trend watching and analysing helps us to make conclusions about how history is going to repeat itself and when.

Apart from trend analysing, statistics plays an important role in collecting, analysing and organising data and information. It helps us in dealing with bombardments of figures, indexes, indicators, rates and percentages. From interest rate fluctuations and inflation to survey results and economic indicators, the need to know how to interpret data and how to use statistical tools is gaining in importance.

Eliminate Counterproductive Concepts

"The world that we have made as a result of the level of thinking we have done thus far creates problems that we cannot solve at the same level as they were created."

Albert Einstein

STRATEGY

Eliminate:	Replace with:
• self-centredness	• outward orientation
• entitlement logic	• self-reward
• movement	• action
• worry	• concern
• symptoms of problems	• fundamental causes
• large-scale efforts	• focused actions
• life by default	• life of conscious choice
• looking in the mirror	• seeing through the window.

13

Continuing Your Education

Break Through The Educational Inhibitions

"In a world that is constantly changing, there is no one subject or set of subjects that will serve you for the foreseeable future, let alone for the rest of your life. The most important skill to acquire now is learning how to learn."

John Naisbitt

In his management classic, *On Becoming a Leader*, Warren Bennis says "Taking charge of your own learning is a part of taking charge of your life, which is *sine qua non* in becoming an integrated person."[21]

Why should you take charge of your own education? The reason is obvious: it lives around us, in the tidal wave of mediocrity and ignorance, and it lives inside of us, because it was implanted there through years of brainwashing in boot camps called schools and universities.

Many people spend sixteen or more years in schools. They studied hard and gave their best, not just because they wanted better jobs, more prestige and higher style of living, but also due to their desire for knowledge and improvement.

However, at one point in their lives or another, many of them realise a disturbing and frustrating truth, which makes them very sad and throws their old systems of values into chaos. It becomes so painfully obvious that most of their education completely missed the point. It wasn't an education at all! It was memorising, fact manipulation, scoring, moulding young minds into very narrow paradigms.

Then the panic strikes them. They feel unprepared for real life! They feel they don't know how to think, because nobody taught them. All they could find in their knowledge bases was dead wood: useless facts, names, titles, figures. Not the methods, principles and ways, just some bits and pieces of information, most of which are irrelevant to their development as human beings and contributing members of society.

FURTHER READING:

If You Want to be Happy, Don't Go to School

Robert Kyosaki's book is a convincing, in-depth and action-orientated work. It's a warning that shouldn't be ignored. The current educational system hampers students' chances for success, it restricts potential and leaves a permanent legacy in young minds. The change is accelerating and our education is not preparing us for such a change. The message is profound: unless we do something about changing the system, our educational and economic decline will continue. This book could save you from wasting time and money in getting a so-called "education" and set you on a course of real, life-long learning.(Kyosaki, R., Excellerated Learning Publishing, San Diego, 1992)

Most of the skills and knowledge that KAIZEN requires is not taught in school. Communication with oneself and others, creativity, problem-solving and decision-making, flexibility, managing change, resourcefulness, conceptual thinking, lateral thinking, intellectual curiosity are hard to find in curricula. They are usually learned in "real" life, through actions, mistakes, victories and defeats. These benefits are brought by experience, but the problem with experience is that it is an expensive way to learn.

153

PARADOX

Conventional education is not conducive to success. It often hinders it. Inhibitions imposed by the educational system are an enormous burden that has to be shed (the sooner, the better) and replaced by new, flexible ways of thinking.

Learn First, Evaluate Later

"Learning is not attained by chance, it must be sought for with ardour and attended to with diligence."

Abigail Adams

Learning the KAIZEN way is learning with an open mind, but with in-built filters and screens. This may sound like a first-class contradiction, but it works quite well in real life. Open mind means that you learn first and evaluate and compare later. It means accepting the fact that others may do some things better than you or know something you don't know (yet). It doesn't mean shielding yourself from new observations by saying: "They do it this way, but my way is also good" or "He does know certain things, but there are some things I know better than him."

Evaluations and comparisons, if done too early in the learning process, inhibit optimum learning. They have their own time and place. Learning with filters and in-built screens means being on a lookout for strategies, tactics, methods and facts that are applicable to your personality, education levels, profession, age, experience and goals. They have to be in line with your aims and have to blend in nicely with your philosophy in life.

Study Successful People

"In actuality, virtually all learning phenomena resulting from direct experience occur on a vicarious basis by observing other people's behaviour and its consequences for them. The capacity to

learn by observation enables people to acquire large, integrated patterns of behaviour without having to form them gradually by tedious trial and error."

Albert Bandura[22]

Learning from others and applying that acquired knowledge towards your self-improvement efforts is the basic way of absorbing know-how and applying it to your situation, to suit your own circumstances. Blatantly copying others in their actions and thoughts is not the way to improvement, but adapting what could be related to your own individuality and applied to problems you need to solve is a prudent practice. It takes special skill to shield yourself from being influenced by values, paradigms and thought processes of others, while accepting the know-how based on those values and methods of operation.

Instead of allowing others to force their ideas and values upon you and accepting those imposed frames of mind and paradigms, KAIZEN advocates a deliberate, conscious and systematic selection of knowledge and experience that others may contribute to your well-being and improvement.

DEFINITION

Eetokotori is the Japanese concept of "taking just the good parts.. It's a recipe on how to copy without really copying.

Keep Learning

"And how many hours a day did you do lessons?" said Alice, in a hurry to change the subject.

"Ten hours the first day," said the Mock Turtle, "nine the next, and so on."

"What a curious plan!" exclaimed Alice.

"That's the reason they're called lessons," the Gryphon remarked, "because they lessen from day to day."

Lewis Carroll, *Alice's Adventures in Wonderland*

Continual growth requires exposure to new experiences, new problems and new knowledge. While interacting with constant changes around us, we often have to learn, unlearn and relearn certain skills, methods and facts, all in a relatively short time span. Learning is your best insurance against becoming obsolete and redundant, not just in your job, but in life.

Learning means that you quit pretending that you know everything, and start finding out about things you don't know. Learning often means getting out of your comfort zone. Should you stay in it, the new information and new developments will bypass you and the hole in your knowledge will grow and grow, until one day you find yourself out of your job, your career, your path to success. It will be taken by somebody who wasn't afraid to try, to make mistakes and to learn about what you left out of your comfort zone – the unknown. In other words, continuous education is a gradual capital improvement of the learner. That learner can be an individual, like you and me, a corporation committed to improvement, or a society.

Continuous learning gives you two basic choices: you can either precede your future developments and events with study or you can follow up on your experiences with study. The first method is about preparation, the second about introspection. With preparation, you anticipate certain experiences and try to learn as much as possible about them beforehand, so you can capitalise on them later, when they eventuate. With introspection, you analyse every experience by asking questions such as "What have I learned?", "How do I feel about that?", "Were my actions appropriate?", etc.

ACTION

Buy yourself a handy pocket-size diary. At the end of a day, write down your answer to the questions: "What have I learned today? How did I make myself better?" No matter how insignificant your daily achievement may seem, write it down and think about it for a while. How much effort did you put in? Why didn't you learn more? What could you change to achieve more in the future?

Draw Your Learning Curve

"Men's business is to know for the sake of living, not to live for the sake of knowing."

Frederic Harrison

Learning, although perceived to be a life-long process, is not a linear function of time; it's got its peaks and lows, plateaux and points of inflection. Human capability to learn and improve is unique amongst living creatures, but grossly under-utilised and neglected. How many times have you heard students or school kids saying at the end of term or after graduation: "Thank God it's over, I'll never touch those books again." How sad and how wrong.

 REFLECTION

*There is one simple Latin truth to be remembered about training and learning: **Non schola sed vita discimus** (We don't learn for school but for life.)*

Apart from having a goal to keep learning, there is another useful activity closely associated with your efforts: monitoring and measuring the progress you make. The learning curve, with its peaks and plateaux is the ideal tool for your self-analysis. Your goal is just to make sure that after each plateau or dip a peak higher than the previous one follows.

What would your learning curve look like? Think about different periods in your life and reflect on how much you learned during each stage. Use the coordinate system below to draw-up your learning curve. Divide the horizontal axis into equal spaces, representing periods of say, three, five or ten years. The vertical axis is qualitative, rather than quantitative. The scale on it doesn't really matter – the relative proportions are what counts.

When you finish, take a critical look at your curve. Is it rising slowly, but steadily, or dipping a bit every now and then? Are there any periods of significant fall? What were the reasons for those periods of decline in the accumulation of knowledge?

The good news is that any gaps in one's education can be filled; the bad news is that in too many cases those gaps are filled with the wrong knowledge.

RECIPE

Never stop learning and never be afraid of making mistakes. This will be your only security for the future.

Ask To Be trained

"I am still learning."
Michelangelo

Today's corporate and small-business environment belongs to people who initiate things. The initiators don't wait to be told what to do or to be trained. They pursue their own ways of growing, learning both on the job and outside it. Initiative is the crucial attitude in the competitive waters.

Learn not only everything about your job, but also as much as possible about other jobs that in some way relate to yours. Cluster your knowledge and skills, develop multi-functional competency. Every time the opportunity presents itself to you, grab it, be it a chance to expand your current duties or to do someone else's job for a while. You will not only make yourself more valuable to your employer – or to your business if you are a small business owner – you'll also increase your future career and business prospects. From that point of view, your capacity to learn will prove to be your ultimate competitive advantage.

Unlearn The "Wrongs" To Be Able To Learn The "Rights"

The act of learning is the act of acquiring knowledge. Once you learn something, that knowledge becomes a part of you. Even if you "unlearn" something, the very act of "unlearning" brings in a new learning experience and takes you further down the learning path.

Take Possession Of What You Read

> *"Self-education is, I firmly believe, the only kind of education there is."*
>
> Isaac Asimov

Reading is the best substitute for first-hand experience. Almost every conceivable situation in human existence has happened at least once before, and there is a high chance that somebody, somewhere, somehow wrote something about it. Reading could be viewed as a tool for making sure we don't repeat other people's mistakes. But reading is much more than that. It a medium for sharing ones thoughts, dreams, ideas, for the transfer of knowledge, for inspiration and consolation.

Active reading is reading with an open mind, with a pen and paper. Active reading shows intent and involvement of the reader through underlining, scribbling questions and comments in the book's margins.

Active reading also means taking possession of the material you are reading, "taking it in", thinking about it, criticising and commenting, rejecting it or finally accepting it as your views or feelings on the subject.

Every book you read will give you something, but it will also demand something from you. Some ask for an undivided attention, others time and effort to persist through their pages until the end, when the real benefits become obvious and when the work's message becomes clear and bonds together all those seemingly disparate concepts or impressions you've encountered along the way.

Read this book with a red pen in your hand. Underline sentences you find important, strike out those you disagree with. Write your thoughts and comments on the margins, ask questions, search for answers.

Use The Power Of Motivational Books

Apart from meeting, associating with and learning from people, reading books is the greatest stimulator and motivator for those who are determined to embark on the path of gradual self-improvement. If a single book can change your entire life, can you imagine the power that will flow to those who read and study many great books?

To get a feeling for such an enormous power, ask your friends, colleagues and acquaintances to give you a list of books they consider to be the most influential ones in their lives. Those books have changed somebody's life already. Read them: they may change yours, too.

 EXERCISE

Think about books you would recommend to others, the books you enjoyed, learned from and, because of them, improved yourself and became a better person.
The books that changed my life:

✍ ....

....

Promote Practical Applications Of Your Knowledge

"One pound of learning requires ten pounds of common sense to apply it."

Persian proverb

KAIZEN promotes practical learning, learning by doing, by trial and error, through a gradual, incremental process. The real, lifelong learning can only be achieved by initiating change, by taking actions and learning from your successes and failures alike. Learning through practical applications of your previous knowledge brings further benefits. Not only will you reinforce what you've learned (by applying it to various situations and problems) but you will also discover more about both your previous and newly gained knowledge. By applying what you know to practical problems you also test your knowledge, which adds value to it and makes it complete, for only tried and applied knowledge is the knowledge that leads towards self-improvement.

Dr An Wang, founder of Wang Laboratories and the author of *Lessons*, concludes his autobiography with the following words:

"The satisfaction of turning an idea into something real never diminishes, and the great gift of change is that it continually replenishes the stock of new ideas that might be brought to life. The thrill of this challenge more than compensates for the setbacks that are the price of learning and growth. There are still many lessons to be learned."[23]

14

Positioning Yourself

Define Your Own Standards

"To affect the quality of the day, that is the highest of arts. Every man is tasked to make his life, even in its details, worthy of the contemplation of his most elevated and critical hour."
Henry David Thoreau, *Walden, or Life in the Woods*

KAIZEN is not simply about achieving goals. It is about self-mastery. Mastering your skills, knowledge, improving your values and raising your standards is self-mastery – the ability to maximise your own potential and to use it for the benefit of yourself and others.

Setting your standards for behaviour and general conduct is the first step towards self-mastery. There are two aims to achieve. First, set a baseline standard for what you expect from yourself and others. Then reprimand yourself for substandard behaviour and reward yourself for better-than-standard behaviour. Don't let others provide that reward/punishment system for you. Your self-improvement and self-actualisation efforts should be carried out according to your own standards, rules and values. Don't strive to conform to the standards others impose on you. Only the standards you feel comfortable with should be self-imposed!

FURTHER READING:

Zen and the Art of Motorcycle Maintenance

The author characterised this book as "an inquiry into values", but this inquiry is only apparently about motorcycle maintenance. In fact, this is a book about quality in its broadest sense, not just the quality of products and service, but also the quality of life. It is impossible to articulate concisely what else this important book is about; the easiest thing to do is to read it carefully.(Robert M. Pirsig, Vintage, London, 1989)

Maintain Standards And Raise Them Gradually

Just as corporations, institutions and society as whole have their own rules, standards, procedures and norms, so does every individual. In business or in society those rules and standards are explicit and in most cases obvious. In corporations they are imposed by management and maintained through discipline and training. In society, they are imposed by governments and maintained by the legal system and police. Individual standards are partly imposed by the outside world (employers, society, other people) and partly self-imposed by individuals themselves.

REFLECTION

Before you can improve your standards and values and build on those foundations, you must have values!

Every time a problem or an issue is resolved, every time we acquire a new bit of information or expand or knowledge or capacity to work, love and live a fuller life, we reach new heights and raise our own standards. Whenever a new level of knowledge, skill, wisdom or understanding is reached, we have to consolidate in our new position.

We say that the improvement achievement has to be consolidated and standardised, to ensure that the new, improved state lasts and doesn't deteriorate back to the original state before the improvement or somewhere in between. KAIZEN is, therefore, based on standardisation.

Recognise And Develop Your Comparative Advantages

> *"A key to self-management is the capacity for self-observation. It is important to realize that self-observation is not the same as overcriticism, judgmentalism, paralysis of analysis. It is rather a consistent monitoring of one's performance from a perspective significantly detached to allow for accurate evaluation."*
>
> Charles A. Garfield, *Peak Performers*

The truth is that all men were *not* created equal. Success in your chosen field, in your career and your relationships, and in life generally, among other factors, depends on how well you know your strengths and how well you develop and use them for your own benefit and that of others. Developing and maintaining a comparative advantage is entrepreneurship. It requires honesty with yourself, seeing things in different lights and from various angles, but most of all it requires relinquishing the status quo.

Comparative advantages are based on distinction, differentiation and originality. Very few qualities and traits you may possess are unique in themselves, but a particular synergetic combination of those qualities that define and describe you certainly is. Those distinctive features and qualities give you a solid base on which to build yourself.

STRATEGY

Capitalise on your comparative advantages; make the best use of them; build your success around them.

If you think you are no different from others and if you don't consider yourself special in any way, but "just another engineer" or "simply an accountant", the law of expectations will make sure you will prove yourself correct and you will turn out to be just that and nothing more.

Don't treat yourself as a commodity. "Commodity thinking" is counterproductive. Substitute it with "maverick thinking". Say to yourself: "I am a maverick, a person who is constantly on the move, who knows what he wants and how to get it. I am a valuable asset to my organisation, to my family and to myself. I am different and special. I don't merely fit into the schemes of things, I actively strive to improve those schemes. I am unique and I will capitalise on that uniqueness."

Make Your Own Openings

One of the beauties of life is certainly its dynamics, the continuous upheaval of forces, ideas, actions and relationships that shape individual and corporate living. Just like sea spiders, who, as they grow in size, constantly search for bigger and stronger shells to inhabit, we also strive and struggle through our days, pursuing happiness and searching for our place in the greater scheme of things. Since more than third of our life is spent at work from which we finance our daily living, it isn't surprising that our success in the corporate and business environment (or the lack of it) shapes our lives more than anything else.

Passivity and mere acceptance of things and people as they appear to be have characterised Western employment philosophy from its very beginnings. High turnover of people, stress, low productivity, strikes, career-changing, the growing small business sector and many other symptoms clearly indicate that all is not well in our corporations.

Rigid structures and inflexible frameworks result in positions dictating people. A job description is written up and the scope of each job decided upon, then a suitable person is searched for. More emphasis is placed on some bureaucrat's preconceived idea about candidates and positions to be filled than on the qualities and potential of real people, who are neatly categorised and boxed into convenient pigeon-holes.

The KAIZEN approach to building teams and organisations is more like gem-cutting and polishing. Instead of cutting individuals down to the standard size, gems of various sizes and weights are combined in the best possible way. The manager is a master jeweller, fitting and refitting those stones to the best of his abilities, acknowledging the fact that the stones themselves change with time and new positions have to be found, or more often created for them.

Positioning yourself as an individual is a matter of finding a suitable opening, or if such opening doesn't exist, in creating one yourself. The opening you should aim for has to allow growth and provide a daily dose of challenge.

Turn Your Losses Into Victories

> *"One is always seeking the touchstone that will dissolve one's deficiencies as a person and as a craftsman. And one is always bumping up against the fact that there is none except hard work, concentration, and continued application."*
>
> Paul Gallico

Short-term pain for a long-term gain is another important principle of KAIZEN philosophy. The Japanese have the maxim *sonshite tokushiro*, which means something like "accept a loss first, and then you can make a profit later."

Knowing how to deal with losses, failures, setbacks, mistakes and imperfections is as important as knowing how to deal with success. Many people have a problem dealing with either of them. They are unable to capitalise on their losses and to turn them into victories primarily because of their inability to admit their own inadequacies. Attribution theory says that when something goes wrong, people blame everything and everybody else, except themselves. They blame the environment, the circumstances, bad luck, their employers, market conditions, competitors, their employees or anything else for that matter. Losers in life blame things and people they have no power to change, instead of talking about the only thing they have the power to change – themselves.

REFLECTION

Discover and unwrap the hidden gifts that come with mistakes, adversities and obstacles – the gifts of learning and the gifts of opportunity. Every difficulty is a challenge, every adversity an opportunity which should be seized and capitalised on.

Develop Your Coexistent Identities

"I contradict myself. I am large. I contain multitudes."
Walt Whitman

Constant improvement and self-renewal is centred around finding your passions in life and following those passions. It also means preparing yourself for future opportunities and adapting to constant change. Balanced self-development efforts nourish and tend the roots of your dormant aspects, not only just various talents, hobbies and skills, but also the multitudes of your personality and various sources of your identity.

Success and satisfaction in life comes from broadness, from involvement in various activities and from exploiting and expressing not only our rational, logical, professional and intellectual side, but also our artistic, playful, creative, intuitive and innovative potential. Limiting our major efforts to one area of achievement is almost necessary to achieving success, but equally important is to develop and keep improving broad, generalist skills. Specialisation tends to limit our behaviour and thinking patterns, while broadness breaks those self-limiting paradigms and patterns and becomes an agent of change, a catalyst which facilitates improvement and allows smoother transitions through different phases of life.

There two equally important motivators for KAIZEN: to get excited about constant improvement, about becoming a better person, and to stay excited despite setbacks and temporary disappointments!

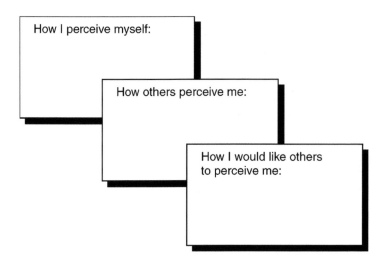

Figure 17. Your perceived identities.

15

Turning Your Dreams Into Goals

Create The Constancy of Purpose

> *"Most gulls don't bother to learn more than the simple facts of flight – how to get from shore to food and back again. For most gulls, it is not the flying that matters, but eating. For this gull though, it was not eating that mattered, but flight. More than anything else, Jonathan Livingston Seagull loved to fly."*
>
> Richard Bach, *Jonathan Livingston Seagull*[24]

Successful individuals, just like successful families or successful companies, are not successful by chance, luck or accident. They have constancy of purpose. They not only meet their present needs, but also plan, think about and focus on the future. They develop a long-term perspective and keep it focused on that future they are creating for themselves.

 FURTHER READING: **Creating Excellence**

Subtitled "Managing Corporate Culture, Strategy and Change in the New Age", this is an "In Search of Excellence"-type manual, which advocates six essential leadership skills – sensitivity, vision, versatility, focus, insight and patience. (C. Hickman and M.A. Silva, George Allen & Unwin, London, 1984)

Tell Yourself A Story Or Two Every Day

"Man is eminently a storyteller. His search for a purpose, a cause, an ideal, a mission and the like is largely a search for a plot and a pattern in the development of his life story – a story that is basically without meaning or pattern."

Eric Hoffer

If you wondered why so many business and self-improvement books use stories and examples to transmit or enforce their messages, the fact is simple. We generally learn much better and are influenced more by short, complete stories than by abstract principles, raw data (facts) and theoretical rules. These little vignettes are concise, complete and easily understood without any need for further explanations. In certain cases, a further emphasis may be placed on certain parts of it, just to reinforce the message or to point out some less obvious aspects.

The best time to tell yourself stories is first thing in the morning, as soon as you get up from bed, and the last thing in the evening, just before you go to sleep. Have you ever noticed how you sing or whistle a tune you've heard in the morning all day long? That tune follows you throughout the day? Have you ever noticed how the bad news you've heard on the early morning news somehow influenced your mood and attitude later in the day?

Some people say about others who may be in a bad and not very cooperative mood that they got up on the wrong foot or got out of the wrong side of the bed. What this really means is that they've started their day with the wrong theme on their mind. The theme you encounter (see, hear, imagine) in the morning will follow you during the day ahead. It will be absorbed by your subconscious mind and will stay there for some time. So, make sure that theme is positive, optimistic and encouraging, instead of depressing, negative or demoralising.

The same applies to the late hours before sleep. The theme that follows you to sleep will occupy your subconscious mind while you are asleep and will shape your emotions and beliefs. Again, make sure it's a positive theme.

Paint Pictures

"The mind never thinks without a picture."
Aristotle

Mental pictures, short stories, symbols, illustrations – our inner thinking and self-talk are nothing else but pictures, symbols, story-books. They help us learn and remember. People with a good imagination generally remember things better and learn faster because they create and combine mental pictures that reinforce the information and knowledge. So, brushes out and let's start painting some mental pictures.

 STORY

When Nikola Tesla, a famous Serbian inventor, one of the greatest the world has known, moved from Budapest to Graz in Austria, he was already well on the way to defining concepts for a poly-phase alternating-current motor. Edison rejected the idea and put his reputation on a direct-current motor, convinced that the AC motor was just Tesla's dream.

One summer afternoon, Tesla was walking with a friend in a park overlooking the city of Graz. The warm tones of the retreating sun reminded him of Goethe's Faust, and he started to recite a passage:

*The glow retreats, done in the day of toil;
It yonder hastes, new fields of life exploring;
Ah, that no wing can lift me from the soil,
Upon its track to follow, follow soaring!*

Then, suddenly, a vision, bright and clear embraced Tesla and the problem of the alternating-current motor was solved! In his excitement, he squatted and started drawing his motor in the dust. Like the Sun, the electric currents, out of phase with each other, raised and ascended in a continuous motion, producing a rotating

171

*magnetic field which would power the rotor and trans-
form electrical energy into mechanical motion. For
Tesla, the dream became a reality and not only the very
foundations of electrical engineering were changed, but
the discovery revolutionised the technical world.*

Plan For Success But Follow Your Dreams

*"A dream is a scripture, and many scriptures are nothing but
dreams."*

Umberto Eco, *The Name of the Rose*

Planning is the symptom of inner control. Having action plans and
contingency plans for the near future, as well as medium and long-
range plans, strengthens our faith in our own ability at least partially
to control future events and have a positive impact on our own future.
Plans are blueprints for action and guidelines for coping with change.
Since change always evokes loss of some kind, plans are guideposts
for maintaining our sense of self and for continuation on our path of
self-management.

The minds of individuals are framed for continuity, not for change.
All instruments and institutions, from the educational system to the
notion of monogamous marriage, prepare us for continuity, stability
and predictability. Plans are our desperate attempts to keep ourselves
chained to the anchors of safety and continuity. The important point
is to recognise that safety does not come from permanency and stability, but from riding the wave of change. Relationships are not permanent: society changes rapidly, laws and institutions change, and so
do people.

Don't attribute too much importance and significance to your
plans. Don't allow them to become your preoccupation; they should
be your system of intelligent response to change, not rigid blueprints
for the future. In other words, don't stick too rigidly to your plans; it
may become necessary to occasionally "murder your darlings."

FURTHER READING: Jonathan Livingston Seagull

Jonathan Livingston was a seagull, but not just an ordinary sort. He was a dreamer. Although he seemed quite ordinary, he always wanted to do more and to achieve more than other seagulls. To fly faster and higher, to achieve mastery and to touch upon beauty were his goals. He dreamed about it, while others in his flock scorned and ridiculed him, angered by his ambitions. Jonathan ignored those who didn't have a dream. He knew the power of dreams and he set out to achieve his own. (Richard Bach)[24]

Learn How To Deal With The Pressure Of Time

Plans and goals are closely related to time management. How we perceive time and how we respond or react to time pressure determines our thinking, behaviour and attitudes and has a major impact on how we manage our resources. Feeling pressured by deadlines is a negative motivator. In the short term it could prompt us to act, but in the long run it's a major cause of anxiety, fear, uneasiness and stress. Our phrases for being under time pressure are the very ones used for people who are about to die: "My time is up", "This will be the end of me!" or "It's hanging over my neck."

RECIPE

Eliminate the word DEADLINE; replace it with TIME-LINE.

Put Your Dreams Into Practice

"We look at it and do not see it; its name is The Invisible.
We listen to it and we do not hear it; its name is The Inaudible.
We touch it and do not find it; its name is The Formless."
                                                    Lao Tzu

Everything exists in two dimensions – first, it is created in your mind, then you make it a reality. Goals are nothing but dreams with a deadline attached to them, dreams taken seriously and translated into reality. As Henry David Thoreau said, "If you have built castles in the air, your work need not be lost; that is where they should be. Now put the foundations under them." This is very true and profound statement. Let that sentiment become your inspiration for creativity, planning and fulfilment of your dreams.

Be careful what you set your eyes upon, because that's precisely what you are going to get. Think carefully about your goals and desires, otherwise you may discover that you were climbing the ladder that was leaning against the wrong wall.

In the space below list your five most beautiful dreams. Describe them, analyse them. What is it that you like about them? How do they make you feel? Why do you think they make you feel the way they do?

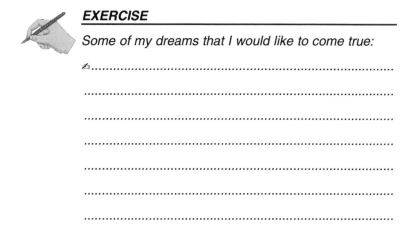

EXERCISE

Some of my dreams that I would like to come true:

✍..

....

....

....

....

....

....

To make your dreams come true you do not have to know what those dreams are, but you do have to come up with an action plan for transforming those dreams into reality. Analyse the conditions that have to be met in order for your dreams to eventuate. Identify the actions you would have to take to make them come true, and also assume what specific kinds of support would you need from others to make your task easier.

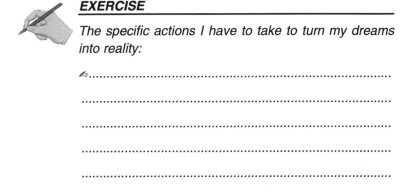

EXERCISE

The specific actions I have to take to turn my dreams into reality:

✍ ....

....

....

....

....

....

....

Buy yourself a big notice-board. Hang it on a wall in your study, kitchen or bedroom, some place where you spend at least a couple of hours every day, where you'll be able to see it clearly for prolonged periods.

Find or draw pictures of your goals. If you dream about owning and running a bookstore, find a photograph of a successful bookshop and pin it onto your board. If a nice two-storey house on the riverfront is among your goals have it prominently displayed on the board so you can keep an eye on it. If your goals are hard to express in material terms, either print them out in large letters or visualise them through material benefits that could follow from achieving them.

Say one of your goals is to learn to speak fluent Spanish in two years' time. This is impossible to convert into a graphic form, but you could display photographs of Spain, South America or Spanish dancers.

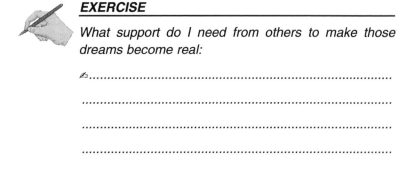

EXERCISE

What support do I need from others to make those dreams become real:

✍ ....

....

....

....

....

....

....

Don't be ashamed of or shy about your goals and dreams. Let others know what they are. People who know you and support you may be able to help you achieve those goals faster and more easily than you would be able to without their help.

Propagate Evangelism

DEFINITION

An evangelist is someone who believes in his or her cause and propagates that cause through integrity, enthusiasm, courtesy and optimism.

Become more than you are, become what you can be. Become a champion, a leader, an ambassador, an evangelist. Leadership doesn't necessarily mean leading others. It primarily means leading yourself. Leadership means different things to different people. To me it means the capacity to create a compelling vision, transform it into action and sustain its pace. Leadership creates a sense of ownership of tasks, work or problems. It provides clear, well-defined expectations, optimal control over one's resources and a sense of direction through guidance and coaching.

- Understand your dream and let it become your living experience.
- Be true to your cause and to others.
- Spread your dream around. Allow others to share it with you.
- Learn from others and help them learn from you.
- Have fun in the process.

FURTHER READING: *Selling the Dream*

Selling the Dream is about evangelism. Evangelism starts with a belief in yourself and your cause and evolves into an integrated approach to sales, marketing and management, equally applicable to both individual and corporate life. Kawasaki shows how to go about defining what is important to you and then convincing others to join your cause and to propagate it even further. His mission statement reads: "I wrote this book to help people spread their dreams and make a world a better place to live." Beware, enthusiasm is very contagious!(Kawasaki, G., HarperBusiness, New York, 1992)

Put Your Self-improvement Plan To Work

RECIPE

Implementing Your Self-Improvement Plan

- *Decide what has to be done*
- *Plan your actions (decide how and when to do it)*
- *Start*
- *Persist with your course of action*
- *Finish*
- *Evaluate the results*
- *Start all over again.*

Set Goals And Objectives

Good goals and objectives should be:

- *Concise.* Keep it simple. When you look at it, each goal has to be self-explanatory.

- *Few in number.* Don't strive for too many things at the same time. Prioritise your goals and concentrate on achieving them one by one.

- *Motivating and challenging.* You should be inspired and motivated by your goals. They should be the ultimate aim of your efforts and source of your strengths.

- *Measurable.* It is very hard, almost impossible, to monitor your progress towards achieving your goals if they cannot be measured or in some other way quantified.

- *Time-framed.* Goals are dreams with deadline. By positioning your goals in time you make them more realistic and measurable. You will be able to monitor your rate of progress towards achieving them.

- *Realistic and relatively easy to implement.* Unrealistic goals are a very common cause of frustration and low self-esteem. Don't be too harsh on yourself. Divide major goals into smaller ones that are easier to achieve.

Use Checkpoints And Milestones

> *"Forecast: To observe that which has passed, and guess it will happen again."*
>
> Frank McKinney Hubbard

Checkpoints and milestones are both used in the assessment of progress in self-improvement effort. Checkpoints reflect the orientation towards process of improvement, while milestones represent the orientation towards achievement or results. These two types of criteria go hand in hand in evaluating your performance against your own standards.

In the self-improvement process, alternatives, options and directions should constantly be evaluated, analysed, planned and followed. The constant feedback on the course you are taking, your goals and the speed in achieving them will minimise side-tracking and help you achieve your aims in the shortest possible time. Checkpoints and milestones are invaluable tools in that process.

In addition to the feedback process, which is corrective in nature (you act upon things that are already happening), the feed-forward process is pro-active. You anticipate events and act in advance in order to prevent some things from happening or to change the course some developments may take.

The concept of critical path is another very useful tool in this process. A critical path is the shortest, the most efficient or the most appropriate course of interrelated actions and steps to take towards achieving a target. There is always some room for error in the critical path. Finding your critical path will help you to move towards your goal even when you get side-tracked and even when things don't go the way they were planned to.

Keep Moving Towards Your Dream

"Ideals are like stars; you will not succeed in touching them with your hands. But like the seafaring man on the desert of waters, you choose them as your guides and following them you will reach your destination."

Carl Schurz

Both as a starting point in your analysis and as a permanent self-analysis tool, some questions should constantly be asked along the way:

- What are my alternatives?
- What are the pros and cons of each alternative?
- What developments could affect my mission?
- What knowledge and skills will I need to complete my mission successfully?
- Where and how do I acquire the knowledge and develop the skills needed?
- How will my choices affect my future?
- What are the critical factors of my success?
- How do I control and achieve those critical factors?

 FURTHER READING: *Pathfinders*

*Pathfinders is a fascinating book whose heroes are people who struggled to overcome adversity and to find heir own paths to well-being. It analyses their beliefs and concerns, their hopes and dreams, but also their errors and mistakes. **Pathfinders** explains why some of us overcome difficulties and adversities while others don't. Through her extensive and detailed research and interviews with hundreds of pathfinders from all spheres of life, Gail Sheehy teaches us how to find uncommon solutions to common problems and simple, common ways to deal with uncommon crises and accidents.(Sheehy, G., Bantam Books, New York, 1982)*

Don't Confuse Being Off The Track With Being Off The Course

"I learned at least this by my experiments. That if one advances confidently in the direction of his dreams, and endeavours to live the life which he has imagined, he will meet with a success unexpected in common hours. He will put something behind and will, pass an invisible boundary."

Henry David Thoreau

In the attainment of your goals and aims, what matters is the general direction you are heading, not the side-tracking and swinging around the main direction. Just as travellers in medieval times travelled through valleys and mountain passages, dry river beds and elevated plains, taking roundabout routes around difficult terrain, swamps and mountains, deep rivers and impenetrable jungles, life often requires temporary or even permanent detours, digressions and changes in direction. The track towards success is not a straight line, a freeway; it rather resembles a long and winding road, with its ups and downs, lefts and rights, sharp turns, tunnels, bridges and fly-overs.

Being on course means a continuous clarification of your values and goals – deciding what is important to you. It also means not forgetting why you are on that track, which often happens when we get entangled in a spider web of problems and small tasks so we lose sight of our priorities.

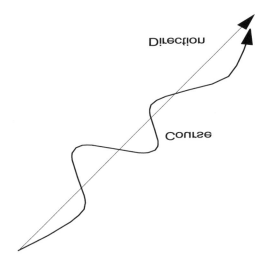

Figure 18. Course and direction – the difference.

16

Searching For Creative Outlets

Foster Creativity

"We have come to think of art and work as incompatible, or at least independent categories and have for the first time in history created an industry without art."

Ananda K. Coomaraswamy

Creativity usually isn't discovering something totally new. In most cases, it is an art based on the concept of relating the normally unrelated. Jules Henri Poincaré, the nineteenth-century French mathematician, argued that new, creative ideas and concepts often result from the convergence of two or more previously unrelated ideas or concepts. This creative synergetic fusion, the discovery that two skills or achievements result in the attainment of other goals and achievements, is the ultimate benefit of creativity.

DEFINITION

Creativity is born from curiosity, struggles to survive under the shadow of complacency and dies from fear and mediocrity.

KAIZEN fosters adaptive creativity, the process of analysing, improving and refining ideas, concepts and knowledge in a systematic, process-like manner. Adaptive creativity analyses the limitations of an individual, corporation or a process, and pushes those limits further through the incremental succession of congruent creative steps – mini breakthroughs with maxi consequences.

Not all creativity is spontaneous. The self-improvement creativity is also deliberate, structured and controlled. The creative process can be deliberately encouraged and cultivated by study, training and broadening one's experience. Maximising one's resources and discovering how those resources could be used better and more efficiently is creativity. Seeking new ways of using old skills is creativity. So is the synergy between knowledge and experience, which results in the ultimate aim: know-how.

To harness your creative powers, following the path of conventional wisdom may not always be enough. Unconventional ways, lateral thinking, brainstorming or intuition cannot be developed or learned mechanically through repetition or self-imposed from the outside. Creativity has to come from within yourself.

 STORY

At an exhibition in Paris, one expert looked over Renoir's paintings and scoffed: "I presume you are dabbling in paint just to amuse yourself?" Renoir looked at the man and replied calmly: "Of course. Once it stops amusing me, I will stop painting."

Get New Ideas By Looking At The Old Ones

"You are told a lot about your education, but some beautiful, sacred memory, preserved since childhood, is perhaps the best education of all. If a man carries many such memories into life with him, he is saved for the rest of his days. And even if only one good memory is left in our hearts, it may also be the instrument of our salvation one day."

Fyodor Dostoyevsky, *The Brothers Karamazov*

There is a view in oriental cultures that ideas never die, but are transformed into new ones in the creativity and discovery process. They may reappear in a slightly changed form, triggered by new developments and inner or outer catalysts. This form of rebirth renews their potential and finds new uses for those old, existing ideas.

Idea recycling is based on mental flexibility and finding new uses for old knowledge. This creative process, as we saw, often results in the discovery of new ways to do old things. Good ideas, productive methods and innovative thinking are scarce commodities and should be conserved and reused as long as they produce worthwhile results.

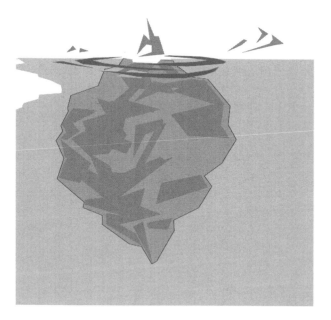

Figure 19. A small idea is often just the tip of a bigger one.

All rejected thoughts and suppressed actions, those that didn't work out for whatever reason, are first-class recycling material. Some occasionally come back to haunt and intrigue us and then disappear into subconsciousness, only to be evoked again, triggered by events, associations and other mechanisms of elicitation.

DEFINITION

Some people look to their past, some discard their past and some carry their past with them into the future. KAIZEN is about recycling the past while creating the future.

Create Opportunity Through Creativity

To give your self-improvement efforts a chance, apart from a determination and an improvement plan, you need opportunities for improvement. Opportunities can be provided to us or created by us. There are many providers of opportunities, and they may broadly classified into two groups: the systems (political, educational, corporate, social, religious, spiritual, etc.) and other people (competitors, customers, co-workers).

KAIZEN is about seizing those opportunities and capitalising on them. It is also about creating your own opportunities when provided opportunities aren't there. Its approach is active, self-reliant, rather than passive and dependent on others.

Created opportunities are fashioned through the use of your own creativity and through your own self-improvement efforts. If seizing provided opportunities is like searching for the windows of opportunity and opening them as wide as possible, created opportunities are like small holes in the walls, created by persistent, diligent and patient hammering, which, after a while, results in knocking bricks out one by one.

If the wall you face has no doors or windows, find a crack and start hammering. Sooner or later a few bricks will be knocked out. Once you make a small hole, it doesn't take much to make it into a bigger one. This is how you create windows of opportunity.

FURTHER READING: *Created in Japan*

This important work analyses Japanese creativity, which transformed a nation of imitators into a world-class innovative power. Tatsuno systematically presents the creative process in a form of a chain of inter-dependent management techniques corporations and individuals use in their search for creative achievements: recycling, search, nurturing, breakthroughs and refinement (KAIZEN).(Sheridan M. Tatsuno, Harper Business, New York, 1990)

Climb The KAIZEN Helix

A circle is a closed curve. No matter how big its radius is, one always gets back to the starting point. The circle is not a curve that describes self-improvement and KAIZEN. Self-improvement is about reaching plateaux. Every new plateau reached is slightly higher than the previous one. There are some falls, naturally – not every endeavour for success results in an improvement – although one may argue that there is a seed of benefit in every failure.

What matters in the end is the upward trend of the unending, incremental process of refinement, improvement and achievement. This is a description of a helix. A circle is a two-dimensional curve; it lacks depth and it leads nowhere. A helix is a three-dimensional, space curve which leads in the general direction of improvement.

DEFINITION

"Quality circles" is not an accurate term; "quality helix" describes the self-improvement process much better.

Sueo Matsubara from the Mukta Institute explains the mandala creativity:

"Creativity is not a one-dimensional circle. Like reincarnation, it is an unending process of refinement and recycling. The mandala

of creativity is really three-dimensional. Each time you go around, the idea should get better and better. Otherwise, you're only going around in circles and going nowhere."[25]

Imagine Your Experiences

"Experience is not a matter of having actually swum the Hellespont, or danced with the dervishes, or slept in a doss-house. It is a matter of sensibility and intuition, of seeing and hearing the significant things, of paying attention at the right moments, of understanding and co-ordinating. Experience is not what happens to a man; it is what a man does with what happens to him."
Aldous Huxley, *Texts and Pretexts*

Our mind is incapable of distinguishing between real and imagined experiences. This amazing statement has been proven by experimental and clinical psychologists and opens a whole new world of self-improvement possibilities and strategies.

 STORY

A teenager, during a visit to Princeton University, noticed a famous figure. Albert Einstein, the father of the theory of relativity, was standing in front of a fountain, tilting his head and moving his hands up and down in front of his eyes. He was trying to synchronise the frequency of his movements with the pearl of droplets to create a stroboscopic effect that would make an illusion that the droplets were stationary. He asked the girl: "Can you do it? Can you see the individual droplets?" As he was leaving, Einstein uttered: "Never forget that science is just that kind of fun."

Get Into The Swinging Mood

Imagine a pendulum, swinging from one side to the other, through elegant, smooth movements. At every point in time, one knows exactly the way the pendulum is going to move, which direction it's going to take. Creativity is a similar oscillating process. It stretches us beyond our limits in an swinging process – we first apply creativity to come up with creative ideas, then we apply our reasoning faculties in an effort to evaluate and analyse those ideas and concepts.

The secret is in not doing both at the same time. Too often we hinder our creative potential by applying the brakes of logic, reason and criticism, while our mind and intellect is in full swing. Just as driving a car by pressing the brake and accelerator pedals simultaneously wouldn't get you very far (the only achievement would be an unexpected windfall for your mechanic), creativity and criticism, when mixed together, don't produce very spectacular results. Although creative thinking and judicial thinking complement each other, they don't particularly like each other's company.

RECIPE

Don't try to be creative and self-critical at the same time. Swing from one mood into the other.

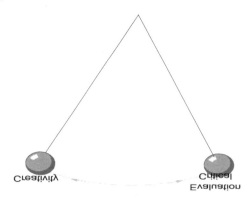

Figure 20. "Creativity" time versus "evaluation" time.

Incubate Your Ideas And Solutions

The power of our subconscious mind lies in the fact that it works even when we don't. Both quantum leaps and gradual improvements are known to result from a period of "incubation", a break in our mental activities during which our subconscious mind searches for answers, ideas and creative solutions. It may be counterproductive to force yourself into finding those answers and coming up with those improvements. Allowing some time for incubation could prove to be a better option.

Many followers of KAIZEN have realised that they've found many solutions to problems and came up with most ideas not while directly dealing with the problems, but after a period in which they withdrew from the issues and allowed them to sublime into the level of subconsciousness. The answers often "popped out" sooner or later.

DEFINITION _____ *Imagineering*

Imagineering is a term apparently coined at ALCOA in the USA some time ago. It summarises the notion that the subconscious mind makes no difference between real and imagined experiences. As a problem-solving, innovative and improvement method, imagineering means allowing one's imagination to run free and then converting those "dreams" into practical solutions through the process of "engineering".

Cultivate Your Creative skills

"First learn to be a craftsman; it won't stop you from being a genius."
    Delacroix's advice to young painters

Creativity is, as we've already seen, a major force that initiates and sustains change and improvement. Creativity which is responsive, focused and fostered through control is the creativity of KAIZEN. The creativity most of us know and use is spontaneous, overwhelming and instinctive. It emerges autonomously when conditions are right and cannot be speeded up or significantly controlled in any way. The cultivated and nurtured creativity of KAIZEN is deliberate and studied. It requires time and effort to cultivate the proper conditions, which then have to be maintained through constant attention, study and feedback. It is highly structured, adaptive and systematic. This kind of creativity refines itself through small improvements, in an incremental manner.

In terms of its applications, KAIZEN creativity is multifunctional – ideas are either developed with various uses in mind or those multiple, new applications are sought later, after an idea is conceived and analysed. Creative urge and longing for their fulfilment lives in all of us. The desire to create, improve, apply or combine knows no ethnic, political, economic or educational boundaries. The only boundaries that exist are in our minds. The desire for significance through creativity is within yourself. It embodies various urges and desires, cravings and hopes, from all aspects life. KAIZEN makes your task of fulfilling that urge easier.

FURTHER READING: *Serious Creativity*

The prolific creator of "lateral thinking" explores myths and misconceptions about creativity and argues that better thinking demands creativity, which is hardly "crazy' or artistic. To de Bono, creativity is serious, logical and systematic, because it uses systematic and deliberate tools. Structures and systems do not limit creative freedom; they channel energy and thoughts. Many structures are liberating. Should you like this book, there are 36 more where it came from.(Edward de Bono, HarperCollins Publishers, London, 1993)

17

Harnessing The Power Of Your Environment

Choose Your Environment

"You are a product of your environment. So choose the environment that will best develop you toward your objective. Analyse your life in terms of environment. Are the things around you helping you toward success – or are they holding you back?"
W. Clement Stone, *The Success System That Never Fails*

Work is one of those words most people dislike. It belongs to the same group as illness, crises, boredom, stress, drudgery, boss, conflict. The reason most people hate work is because they find it an unpleasant experience. In many cases what makes them think that way and see their situation in that light is not, as the so-called Theory X suggests, that people naturally hate work and are basically lazy, uncommitted and unreliable, but because of the climate they work in, because of the work environment that surrounds them.

Work environment is just one example of how our surroundings affect our feelings, our behaviour, and, ultimately, our achievements. Obviously, to neutralise the negative influences of your environment and to harness the positive ones, you should choose the environment that will be the most conducive to your aims, goals, purpose and mission in life. Select the environment that will help you in your self-improvement and self-actualisation efforts, not the one that will make it difficult for you by dwarfing those efforts.

If your aim is to become and act as a professional, provide yourself with professional working conditions. Changing the structure and the nature of your immediate surroundings, as well as the broader environment, is likely to be the major factor in your self-improvement and self-actualisation efforts.

RECIPE

Continuous improvement requires you not just to adapt to your environment, but also to change that environment as much as possible to suit you.

Capitalise On Your Surroundings

By improving your ability to cope with your environment in a flexible and resourceful manner and by integrating the qualities of that environment into your living philosophy, you harness the benefits the environment brings and foster self-growth and personal satisfaction.

The Random House Dictionary defines *telesis* as "the deliberate, purposeful utilisation of the processes of nature and society to obtain particular goals." The concept is very close to stewardship – a masterful management of one's resources. Both are entwined in the process during which man and his environment interact with each other and shape each other.

EXERCISE

List the three most important factors, people or developments you think may affect your life in the next five years:

✍..

....

....

....

....

Use KAIZEN As A Bridge Between Your Inner And Outer World

We live in two parallel worlds. Reality exists beyond ourselves as individuals; it exists regardless of whether we do or don't exist. One of the aims of self-improvement is to get to know this world, to live it to its full potential and to change it by making it a better place. We share this world with others and interact with others through it as a medium.

The other world is the world that exists only because we exist. It's the individual's world, the world with its own rules, feelings, boundaries and sensations.

KAIZEN originates in such an inner world, within ourselves, but is both inner- and outer-oriented. On both the personal and social level, KAIZEN signifies the importance of improving the ability of inward contact with oneself, which is a catalyst for personal growth. Self-improvement requires a perspective of knowledge, methods and tools for lifelong learning and improvement.

KAIZEN therefore builds on both inner and outer world dynamics, in stark contrast with the prevailing culture which is dominated by competitiveness, consumption, status and material possessions, all symbols of an materialistic outlook. The outer-oriented culture we live in signifies a materialistic attitude in evaluating and judging our life experiences. It places far greater importance on the outer improvement than on the inner mastery, possibly because the inner world is still perceived as something mystical, unreal, intangible and vague.

PARADOX

Self-improvement is manifested outside ourselves, but has to originate and be sustained and promoted from within.

Find A Cure For The "Impossible Syndrome"

"All men plume themselves on the improvement of society, and no man improves."

Ralph Waldo Emerson

The losers in life have their favourite words and tend to use them often. Please delete these words and phrases from your vocabulary, and, more importantly, from your mind:

- Impossible!
- Can't ...
- If only...
- Difficult!
- We've always done it this way.

Words shape our emotions and our way of thinking. Emotions and thinking patterns in turn influence and shape our beliefs and paradigms, which have a direct impact on our actions. Therefore, words are actions and should be treated as such – with respect and caution.

DEFINITION

The "Impossible Syndrome":I can't. You can't. We can't. They can't. Therefore, it's impossible.

Think Small, Think Simple

"Events of great consequence often spring from trifling circumstances."

Livy

Thinking small and simple may sound derogatory in a society used to complex concepts, large-scale projects, investments, take-overs, yet thinking small is a concept that involves both the inner and outer worlds of an individual or corporation. It means having a purpose that will serve both as a guiding light and a measuring yardstick in avoiding clutter, irrelevant facts, ideas, empty possessions and futile efforts. Thinking small and simple also means also paying due attention to little things, in which the spirit of success lives. These are the very details in which the enemy lurks, small issues that could turn into big problems.

In his book *Created in Japan*, Sheridan Tatsuno illustrates the concept of miniaturisation, which is possibly Japan's best-known and most outstanding form of creativity, the concept that influenced not only Japanese art, but also Japanese industry, the character of people and their way of thinking.

> *"Take, for example, miniature Japanese wood carving, or **netsuke**. In the Kamakura period (1185-1333), Japanese men wore small wooden hanging objects, or **sagemono**, to secure small purses to their sashes. Those objects were adorned with intricately carved **netsuke** figures of Buddhas, wild animals, and natural scenes. By the Edo period (1600-1868), **netsuke** had risen to the level of high art and was worn by samurai and merchant classes alike. A symbol of personal wealth and creative taste, **netsuke** became so pervasive that gradually the Japanese became accustomed to the idea of carrying around miniature products."[26]*

RECIPE

Don't just be a "big thinker", who only thinks about concepts and important issues. Sometimes it pays to be a "little thinker", too, paying attention to details and minor points. Always remember that a small hole can sink a big ship.

Resist Distractions

The environment of modern urban society is a noisy one. By noisy we don't literally mean the level of acoustic noise, but the fact that our minds are constantly being bombarded with information, pictures and messages of all kinds. Our minds are facing information overload. This burden of unneeded, unwanted and often useless information has to be dealt with and that itself constitutes a waste of our precious resources.

Continuous improvement relies on information which can be used, acted upon or created for the benefit of an individual or a society. It doesn't rely on the quantity of information but on quality information. Junk has to recognised and screened out. Distractions have to be fought and avoided.

 REFLECTION

Fight or avoid distractions.

Use The Right Tool For The Right Job

"The tools of the mind become burdens when the environment which made them necessary no longer exists."

Henri Bergson

KAIZEN is not just about inventing new tools for improvement, it is also about better use of the tools you already have. If the tools you are using fail to produce any results, change your tools. If they produce results you didn't expect, you may consider changing your expectations. The greatest delusion of the human mind is hoping for better results while doing the same unproductive things over and over, without being aware of the context of those actions. The message is simple: don't automatically change the tool you are using – the way you are using it may be wrong!

 STORY

Thor Hammer Co. Ltd manufactures hammers in various shapes and sizes, made from various materials and designed for various purposes. There are "ball-pein" and "cross-pein" hammers, steel-shafted claw hammers with

heat-treated and polished heads, soft-faced hammers which can deliver powerful blows without damaging the finished work. "Copper and hide" hammers with copper and rawhide faces are used for a firm but resilient blow which will not mark materials, while "dead-blow" hammers, with shock-absorbent rubber grips and replaceable screw-in nylon faces, are used in positioning of precision parts and shaping of sheet-metal work.

Learn Foreign Languages And Customs

"The difference between a mountain and a molehill is your perspective."
Al Neuhart, *Confessions of a S.O.B.*

Our age is an age of globalism. The political, cultural and economic systems are integrating at an unprecedented pace. Learning in such an environment is, above all, based on exposing oneself to new ideas, adopting new ways of thinking and making an effort to understand others. Becoming proficient in foreign languages is a first step in that process. It helps us to understand the psychology, history and tradition of others, because an understanding of customs, culture, tradition, thought processes, rituals, formalities and religion (among other things) is so important in doing business with foreigners or even simply socialising with them.

Travelling abroad or living in a foreign country changes one's perspective, one's outlook on the world and one's stance in relation to the surrounding environment. When you shift your vantage point, your perspective changes and, as a consequence, your perception of reality is immediately altered. It's like looking at the world through a new pair of eyes. Ideas, concepts, information or problems have to be put into context and looked at from various perspectives (as we have already seen in "Change Your Spectacles"). Transforming your experiences into lifelong learning is possible only through regular alteration of your perspective and viewpoint.

18

Achieving Success Through Others

Help Others Help You

"Move forward in harmony with the world."
A message on a factory wall in Japan

KAIZEN is a mind set. It is way of relating to others as well as to yourself. It is an overriding strategy that holds together your beliefs, habits, frames of mind, actions and thoughts – a thread that links all your resources and focuses them on maximising achievements through better use of those resources.

KAIZEN is also an improvement in rendering services to others, understanding their views and opinions and respecting those views. It is one of the basic principles of living, based on a philosophy that if we provide a valuable service to others, positive results and benefits, both tangible and intangible) will follow sooner or later.

Learn Kikubari

*"I have bought
Golden opinions from all sorts of people."*
William Shakespeare, *Macbeth, 1.vii.44*

Kikubari is a Japanese concept that deals with and synergetically encompasses Western concepts of empathy, service and win/win philosophy. It is about being sensitive to the concerns of others and about making it possible for them to feel appreciated, helped and supported. It also epitomises responding to the needs of others and trying one's best to satisfy those needs for mutual benefit. This often includes going out of your way to help others and intuitively responding to the unstated.

More on *kikubari* can be found in a book *Kikubari no Susume* (May I Suggest Kikubari), by Kenji Suzuki.

STORY

Airline passengers in Japan are referred to as "okyakusama" (guests). The training of hostesses takes about five months and, apart from standard topics such as serving food, safety demonstrations and cabin luggage handling, involves many aspects of a typically Japanese culture.

*The art of flower arranging ("ikebana") is studied and practised, the tea ceremony is brought to a perfection and many hours are dedicated to practising gracious movements in national costume. Hostesses are known for their **miyabi** (refined elegance) and **wabi** (quiet taste). The ever-improving standard of services through KAIZEN philosophy is high on the management's priority list.*

Renounce The Concept Of Scarcity

One of the key principles in economics is scarcity. It teaches us that resources available to humans are scarce and exhaustible. While this may be true for minerals, land and common goods, it certainly isn't true for human potential. The scarcity mentality created by those teachings cannot differentiate between the marketplace and the individual's resources. Once accustomed to the scarcity way of thinking, we falsely assume many things that restrain us from achieving success through others, from helping ourselves by helping them. The typical examples of such false thinking:

- By giving some of my power away, I'll lose it forever.
- By giving important information away, I will lose control and help my competitors.
- By sharing my profits, my slice of the pie will become smaller.

A scarcity-oriented society also exerts a great influence on people, the majority of whom become "collectors", with a philosophy oriented towards having things and accumulating material wealth. They seldom realise that doing things that help them grow and making a difference in life are what matters, not owning pieces of somebody else's achievement.

 RECIPE

Replace win/lose mentality with the win/win frame of mind.

KAIZEN recognises two paradigms: potential scarcity and potential abundance. Having one or the other is a matter of choice. You can have either of them, if you so wish. Accepting the notion about abundance is one of the cornerstones of KAIZEN. Through knowledge, stewardship and innovation, KAIZEN teaches us to achieve more with less, to leverage and compound what we have, sustain achieved benefits and flexibly and elegantly create the outcomes we desire.

 STRATEGY

Losers move within boundaries; champions move the boundaries.

Create Alliances, Support Groups And Partnerships

"Here lies a man who knew how to bring into his service men better than he was himself."
Andrew Carnegie's epitaph

Invest time and effort in people who can teach you something or who can make you feel better, more positive or more determined. Stop expending your time on those who are unable or unwilling to grow with you. Align yourself with people who share the same values, who strive towards similar goals. Work for companies who foster the values you stand for. There is nothing more humiliating and more demeaning to the human spirit than going to work every day for an employer whose ethics, values and standards are different or conflicting with your own. You cannot simply leave your standards behind when you walk through that door.

The same applies to growth. If your company grows faster than you, capitalise on it. Learn as much as you can, try to catch up, use it as a motivator, align yourself with its growth. If you grow faster than your job or your company, change company or find another job with more room for growth and development. Change your environment once it becomes a limiting factor. Find a new breeding space.

Make Synergism Work For You

"No matter how much work a man can do, no matter how engaging his personality may be, he will not advance far in business if he cannot work through others."
John Craig

Synergism (also called synergy), briefly explained, is a philosophy that claims that two and two, if put together in an innovative and creative way, will not add up to four, but to five or more. The basic idea is that interactive, focused, coherent and synchronised actions of two or more people, if properly managed and directed, are far greater than the simple sum of all individual efforts.

Synergy is about aligning individual purposes in order to serve the common aim. Instead of working at their own pace and in their own directions, the personal power of individuals is channelled and focused, individual "specialities" are blended together in a process which results in complementing each others' skills and "covering up" each others' weaknesses.

 REFLECTION

Synergistic concepts:

* *Common aim*
* *Shared vision*
* *Consistency of purpose*
* *Complementing skills and effort*
* *Alignment of directions, values and actions*
* *Mutual motivation and support.*

Make Service Your First Priority

Service is everything we do for or give to others. Service to our employers, our customers and colleagues, our families and friends is the core of our existence. "No man is an island, entire in itself," said the poet John Donne. Service is that bridge between your island and the mainland of others.

To serve others we must be committed to providing the best service possible. Loose commitment does not exist in KAIZEN. Commitment to service has to be unequivocal. The experience of visiting a Japanese shop is quite different from what we are used to calling service. Japanese call it *anshinkan* – literally translated as "a peace of mind." In *Gaishi – The Foreign Company in Japan*, T.W. Kang describes a typical supermarket experience:

> *"Everything about the supermarket is designed to reassure the customer that the store is reliable and trustworthy; its goods are*

fresh and of high quality, its operations are efficient and convenient, and its service is accommodating. The customer is left with the perception that his or her needs will be satisfied."[27]

EXERCISE

List at least 20 ways you use to show respect for others:

✍ ....

....

....

....

....

....

....

....

....

....

....

....

....

....

....

....

....

....

....

....

....

....

Service isn't just doing what's expected of us; it means a complete frame of mind, a whole new mindset. Don't just meet the expectation of others, exceed them. The element of surprise is very powerful. Deliver more than you promise and deliver it every time. When people get from you less than they expected, they feel cheated. When they get more, they feel obligated and indebted. They will come back for more. This applies in sales, in personal relationships, in careers and in any other aspect of life.

 STORY

Joe Girard, born in a poor Detroit neighbourhood in 1928, sold newspapers, delivered Pepsi and polished shoes. His father told him he would never amount to anything. In 1963, Joe became a Chevrolet salesman. In 15 years he sold 13,001 vehicles, 1425 in 1973 alone. The Guinness Book of World Records named him the world's greatest salesman.

How did he do it? "I heard it over and over again – you must love what you're involved in," Girard insists. "If you do, it shows in your eyes, your personality, your movements. If you have that enthusiasm, you can close anybody."[28]

Girard had a unique personal message for his buyers. When he sold a car, he told them they bought two things: 'You've bought a beautiful car and you've bought Joe Girard."

Deploy Yourself For Your Own Cause

"First and foremost, find out what it is you're about, and be that. Be what you are, and don't lose it ... It's very hard to be who you are, because it doesn't seem to be what anyone wants."

Norman Lear

When you rely on others and depend on them in one way or another, your destiny, your success and your reputation are largely in someone else's hands. Self-improvement doesn't necessarily mean that working with others, helping others or getting help from others is of secondary importance. It signifies the prudence and benefits of self-reliance and self-management.

REFLECTION

Dependency on the opinions of others is an impediment to self-mastery and constant improvement. Freedom of expression and freedom of choice are not possible if you value the opinion of others more than your own.

Some people, usually when reflecting upon their lives and when faced with their own mortality, realise what has been done to them. They suddenly realise that the careers, companies, ideas or people they've dedicated their efforts and lives to are not giving them anything in return. The seed of suspicion of being manipulated, used and exploited then starts to germinate into an overwhelming feeling of frustration, anger, disillusionment and revenge.

They realise that for many years they have been deployed and used for ideas, motives, profits and benefits that were not theirs. All their knowledge, energy, enthusiasm and, most importantly, time have been wasted because they failed to produce tangible benefits for them-selves. They sowed, but someone else reaped. This is a very impor-tant notion. It is one of the cornerstones of this book: self-deployment for one's own benefits. Please keep this always on your mind.

RECIPE

Deploy yourself, for your own good. Don't allow others to deploy you for their own purpose and benefit.

Don't Turn Back To Those Left Behind

"The best index to a person's character is (a) how he treats people who can't do him any good, and (b) how he treats people who can't fight back."

Abigail Van Buren

Improving yourself, no matter how gradually, almost always means changing yourself, your views and personality. You will expand your personal identity, you will identify yourself with different things and ideas. You will find new perspectives not only on your past, but also on your present and future and those perspectives will also change your relations with others. Former relationships, support mechanisms and certainties will all be redefined and both you and those around you will have to redefine various aspects of your old self.

Some people you know, be it your friends, relatives, co-workers or even your own family, will be threatened by the course of your changes and by where that improvement course is leading you. Many will not be prepared to follow your example and join you on your journey towards self-betterment. Your growth will leave many of the people you care about behind.

At such a point you will have to make a crucial decision: to proceed regardless or conform to those around you and maybe try to change them to your way of thinking and make them grow with you. The problem with the latter option is that you would again be dependent on others and that everybody must ultimately decide for themselves; the drive for self-improvement has to be within oneself – you cannot instil it into others. You can encourage it, direct it and harness it, but you cannot implant it.

Have An Open-Door Policy

"I have been having some trouble with a flower," said the little prince.
"Ah!" said the snake.

And they were both silent.
"Where are the men?" the little prince at last took up the con-
versation again.
"It is a little lonely in the desert ..."
"It is also lonely among men," the snake said.
Antoine de Saint-Exupery, *The Little Prince*

Champions listen to what others have to say. They listen actively and learn from every encounter, every interaction with others. Let others teach you things you don't know and confirm those you do. Accept everyone as your equal, as a person you can learn from. Take the good parts from everybody, learn about the bad ones, so you can recognise them within yourself and fight against them.

Surround yourself with people who aim to grow, so you can grow with them. Associate with positive, focused and resourceful people who can teach you how you can become positive, focused and resourceful. The germs of self-improvement are very contagious.

STRATEGY

Tell others: "I want you to improve, so I can improve with you!"

Understand And Harness The Emotions Of Others

"We can only have the highest happiness, such as goes along with true greatness, by having wide thoughts and much feeling for the rest of the world as well as ourselves."
George Eliot

The true mastery lies in understanding the emotions of others and in using the latent power of those emotions to achieve worthwhile and mutually beneficial goals.

Simply using the emotions of others for your own purposes is called exploitation and manipulation. Using those emotions to propagate certain causes, new ideas, new or better ways of doing things may be called evangelism. Using the emotions of others in a way which facilitates their decision-making, provides them with the tools and knowledge needed for action and embodies those feelings in a suitably constructive frame of mind is called empowerment.

Empowering others is a synergetic concept, where the value of the whole created from the individual components exceeds the sum total of the components of that whole. Empowering others comes from understanding them, knowing what motivates them, what their hopes, dreams and plans are, helping them to capitalise on their strengths and minimise their weaknesses. We call it empathy; American Indians refer to "walking in another person's moccasins"; the Japanese talk about *haragei*.

DEFINITION

Haragei *(Jap.) the art of getting inside other people, from* **hara***, stomach, and* **gei***, art. Body-snatching KAIZEN style.*

Create Excitement

Excitement and action go hand in hand. The emotion of excitement has the power to turn any adversity into a challenge or problem into an opportunity. Excitement is a fuel of excellence and continuous improvement. Excitement in KAIZEN does not come from the philosophy itself, for there is nothing really exciting in its concepts. It comes from the fact that by taking those steps towards improvement one becomes empowered to easily handle negative emotions, solve problems, handle crises and take small but consistent and decisive actions towards the aim.

The excitement creates a paradigm shift in ourselves and others: it channels positive emotions into a powerful stream and reduces the flow of negative ones into a tiny trickle.

STRATEGY

To succeed at anything in life, you first have to achieve two things – create excitement in yourself, then in others.

Become An Ambassador

An ambassador doesn't necessarily represent a country or a nation. As an ambassador, your represent your company, your employer, your own business or yourself. You represent all you stand for in every action you take and in all your dealings with others.

DEFINITION

Being an ambassador:

- *always doing, looking and acting your best*
- *representing your business, your family, your country and yourself to the best of your abilities*
- *promoting what is good, just, decent, fair and progressive; helping those less fortunate than yourself*
- *striving to maximise your contribution towards a common good.*

Give Others The Gift Of Love

To improve yourself is not an end in itself; it just a means that could lead you towards the ultimate aim. All too often, as we strive towards becoming smarter, broader, stronger, we lose sight of things that are important, thinking that the ultimate aim is to do more and accomplish more. *No.* The only thing that matters at the end is how much love we give to others.

Love is not just an emotional or sexual concept. Love is everything we do for others, everything we teach others and share with them.

Love is me writing this book right now, hoping that it may help you give more of *your* love to others. Love is sharing one's knowledge with others, risking one's life to save others, helping others achieve their goals.

In his book *One Person Can Make a Difference*, Gerald Jampolsky says about love: "Gifts of love can never be measured. When we are giving love there are no small or large gifts. All gifts of love are the same – boundless, complete, and non-exclusive, always extending out toward others, and always expanding without limitations."[29]

STRATEGY

Send a note to those you love and thank them for being an important part of your life. Send a similar thank-you note to your enemies and observe how many of them will change their attitude towards you.

19

Fighting The Enemies Of Continuous Improvement

Accepting the Status Quo As "The Best I Can Do"

If you feel there is no possibility of improving yourself, you'll prove yourself right. Likewise, if you feel there is a plenty of room for improvement, you'll find that room and you'll prove yourself right again.

DEFINITION

Champions want to change things. They want to see things happen. Losers just want to talk about things.

Status quo, although it may not seem so at times, can easily be changed, for better or for worse. Both processes are self-compounding, self-perpetuating. Smaller improvements lead to bigger ones. A seemingly insignificant deterioration worsens until it reaches irreversible proportions.

Mediocrity is one of the worst enemies of KAIZEN, an enemy that shouldn't be ignored or underestimated. Mediocrity is a direct consequence of inaction, complacency and procrastination. I would like to appeal to you now to make fighting against mediocrity your personal philosophy in life. Reject mediocrity, pursue it and expose it, fight against it relentlessly. Demand a lot, from yourself and others; refuse to settle for the inferior or second-rate. Don't tolerate violence, rudeness, dishonesty, fraud, corruption, abuse, discrimination, crime. Fight injustice and evil thoughts and actions with all your weapons.

Confusing Constant Improvement With Perfectionism

> *"You will begin to touch heaven, Jonathan, in the moment that you touch perfect speed. And that isn't flying a thousand miles an hour, or a million, or flying at the speed of light. Because any number is a limit, and perfection doesn't have limits. Perfect speed, my son, is being there."*
> Richard Bach, *Jonathan Livingston Seagull*[30]

Constant improvement is *not* about perfectionism. Although one may argue that by constantly improving ourselves we certainly approach the ideal we are striving towards, there is nothing perfect in life and that ideal we set as our goal is not perfect either. Perfectionism actually has the potential to seriously hamper our constant improvement efforts.

The world we live in and the lives we lead change constantly and never exhibit the qualities that could be described as perfect. We have to learn to live with change, uncertainty and ambiguity. We have to get accustomed to those principles and embrace them as the only certainty. Some problems and issues are to be solved and improved, some are to be lived with. Perfectionists try to improve everything and are often frustrated when things don't turn out as they want them to. In that respect, it's better to be a compromiser than a perfectionist. Compromisers achieve realistic results, time and resources permitting; perfectionists achieve nothing.

STRATEGY

There is always some room for improvement.Nothing is perfect and everything can be improved in some way.

Perfectionism is a spectator sport. Self-improvement is not. If you strive for perfection, you spend more time watching what other people do or say so you could find the secret of delivering perfect results (which is the trademark of losers) than taking real actions that bring real, although slightly imperfect results (which is the signature of champions).

Searching For Immediate Results And Short Cuts

"Dear God, I pray for patience. And I want it right now."
                                        Oren Arnold

"I know why there are so many people who love chopping wood. In this activity one immediately sees the results," once said Albert Einstein. The activities associated with continuous improvement seldom lead to immediate results – KAIZEN is about success through patience. Nothing is oriented towards short-term gains, everything you do should be geared towards long-term success. If you buy a business and want to make a quick profit, your main aim is to build up the figures, increase the turnover and profits as quickly as possible so the books look good, then sell out. With the long-term orientation, your main aim is to build strong foundations to improvement and success for creating your own future.

Patience, KAIZEN-style, is the knowledge of how and when to deny yourself, and the willpower to see it through. Patience is therefore a matter of controlling yourself, of proving to yourself and others that you are there to stay, to finish what you've started, to be an achiever, not a quitter. Patience empowers you to develop an integrated approach to problem-solving and stewardship, both of which require orchestrated and coordinated use of your skills and resources.

Clinging To Strategies That No Longer Work

"The words of truth are always paradoxical."
Lao Tzu

The paradox of self-improvement KAIZEN-style is in its continuity and sustainability. As we have seen so far, incremental, manageable self-improvement efforts and tasks are the backbone of KAIZEN. Yet there is no guarantee that the methods, actions and ideas that produced positive improvements yesterday will produce equally positive results tomorrow. If your beliefs, actions and efforts become outmoded and counterproductive (and they often do) instead of bringing benefits and moving you towards your goals, they may achieve quite the opposite!

The paradox of KAIZEN is that improvement emerges from incremental, cohesive succession of right moves, which have to be sustained and continued, but only if they lead in the right direction. If they don't, they have to be discontinued and other improvement avenues have to be found.

Strategies for improvement should not be carved in stone, nor should one become blinded by overcommitment to those that don't produce the desired results. The type of commitment KAIZEN requires is a commitment to its broad philosophy and a strategic trust towards self-improvement, not to particular ideas, actions and methods that may or may not bring desired benefits. It isn't easy to give up strategies and ways of thinking and doing that have served us so well in the past. A commitment to being on the lookout for actions that don't produce desired results and for strategies that no longer work is a commitment to constant improvement.

The typical reaction of a human being under stress, facing problems or experiencing extreme hardship, is to continue using the same methods, thinking the same way and doing more of the same as before, just trying harder and harder. KAIZEN teaches the often more beneficial way of doing the same things differently or doing completely different things.

STRATEGY

Just as a trapped fly constantly flies towards a lit window, we often stubbornly charge in the direction of single leads, forgetting that an idea could be very dangerous if it's our only one and that the guiding light could also blind us from seeing other options and possibilities. The strategy of a cockroach is fundamentally different from that of a fly. A cockroach will explore the perimeter, defining the space and locating the exit, not blindly assuming that a source of light points to it, like a fly does.

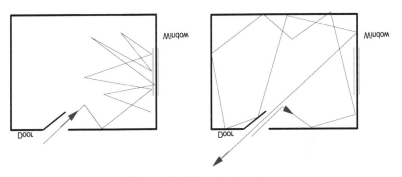

Figure 21. Two strategies.

RECIPE

The crucial skill in sustaining your success is to recognise strategies and actions that no longer work and to replace them with ones that do.

Not Seeking Out Criticism

Don't wait for others to provide you with feedback – it may never happen. Find out what others think of your efforts and achievements.

What is needed are honest and unbiased opinions, which are always difficult to obtain since most people are reluctant to criticise others and speak their mind openly. This is why "reading between the lines" in situations of this kind becomes an indispensable tool for understanding the real meaning of praise or criticism (or a mixture of both).

Hesitation Or Unwillingness To Attack Traditional Ideas

RECIPE

Be an iconoclast. Attack the old, but only if you have something better in sight. Bringing down the old just for the sake of destroying it is barbarism. Bringing down the old for the sake of present or future benefits is called innovation.

Accidents happen, just as circumstances change. The losers become victims of circumstances and suffer from accidents. The winners to become the victors of circumstances and take advantage of accidents. Just as the winners consciously make an effort and *choose* their response to adversity, the losers unconsciously *choose* their reactions to it. The reality is the same for both. The setbacks are equally real and serious. But the outcomes are amazingly different.

Trying To Change Everything

The self-improvement strategy outlined in *KAIZEN and You* is realistic. It recognises that our improvement is limited to certain manageable areas, that our choices and opportunities are not unlimited. There are factors outside one's control and there are constraints that mark the boundaries and impose limits on our manageable factors. One has to identify those factors and constraints, assess to what extent they impact on the choices one could make and how to manage those factors and constraints in order to maximise the area over which control can be established.

Providing The Right Answers To The Wrong Questions

"The uncreative mind can spot wrong answers, but it takes a creative mind to spot wrong questions."

A. Jay

KAIZEN identifies two requirements for any solution to be found, for any issue to be resolved, for any analysis to be carried out. The first is to ask the right questions. The second is to find the right answers. Asking the right questions is about definition, about putting things in perspective and about identifying core issues. Finding the right answers is about the proper ways of dealing with those well-defined issues.

RECIPE   **The enemies of KAIZEN**

- *Complacency*
- *Procrastination*
- *Suppressing negative issues*
- *Problem avoidance*
- *Lack of long-term plans and strategies*
- *Using the wrong tools and methods*
- *Short-term thinking*
- *Inability to postpone immediate gratification*
- *Using strategies that no longer work*
- *Unwillingness to attack traditionalism.*

Conclusion

Make These Words Your Own

Once you've studied the concepts of continuous improvement outlined in this book, tried them in practice, modified them to suit your circumstances and accepted them as your living philosophy, as your guideposts towards success, they will become truly yours. They will become your new reality, new frame of mind, inseparable from your thoughts and actions.

Take a pen and a paper and write down thoughts, sentences and techniques outlined in *KAIZEN and You* which work you. Write them down in your own words, the way you feel comfortable with them. Make them truly yours. Don't worry, I won't sue you for plagiarism. The words in this book are yours, should you need them; that's why they are here.

Make This Book an Annual Event

Reading a book is one of the best ways to learn and to increase your level of awareness. Reading a book more than once and making it a regular event is the best way to keep learning and exploring its depths. Make a commitment to read *KAIZEN and You* again in six or twelve months' time. Put a note in your diary or mark your calendar. The trouble with us humans is that we forget. Refresh your memory.

Every time you read a book, don't just read between the lines. You should also write between them. Write in the margins, stick in notes and reminders. Whatever you write will become a part of your book and give it a new life, a particular meaning that is yours and nobody else's. You have to understand that although this book is just a medium through which you and I communicate, it will also help you to communicate with yourself, to open your inner channels of thought and communication. The communication between us is a two-way process. You have to question me, argue with me, supplement my thoughts with yours.

Mortimer Adler, writer, editor, philosopher and educator, argued that the full ownership of a book is not a simple result of a purchase. "Full ownership comes only when you have made it a part of yourself, and the best way to make yourself a part of it is by writing in it."[31] In 1940, Adler's *How to Read a Book: The Art of Getting a Liberal Education* was a best-seller.

 STORY

Ivo Andric, the Yugoslav novelist and Nobel prize laureate, was once asked by a young screenwriter if he would agree for one of his novels to be shortened for the purpose of making a movie. Andric replied, "Son, shorten as much as your heart desires, but I beg you, don't add anything!"

Share It With Others

If you like *KAIZEN and You*, tell your friends about it; lend it to them (just make sure you get it back, because you'll need it regularly). Become an evangelist for the philosophy of constant self-improvement. Form a club, a debating group. Read other books on similar topics. Compare them. Try various methods of self-improvement. Write your own book and send me a copy. If more people were writing books and listening to what others have to say, there would be less misery and much, much more happiness in this world.

Reward Me With Your Feedback

If you have something to say to me, something to share or something to chat about, I will be glad to hear from you. Since I like receiving faxes, send me on or more. My fax number is +619-368-1600.

> **Thank you for reading this book and for giving me the opportunity to share my message with you.**

Bibliography

"Those who don't read good books have no advantage over those who can't."

Mark Twain

Crosby, P.B., *Quality is Free*, Mentor, New York, 1980.

Dauten, D., *Taking Chances,* Newmarket Press, New York, 1986.

De Bono, E., *Tactics: The Art & Science of Success*, Fontana/Collins, London, 1989.

Faller, F.R., *Recreating Yourself*, Thorsons, London, 1992.

Garfield, C., *Peak Performers*, Avon Books, New York, 1986.

Hopkins, T., *How to Master the Art of Selling,* Warner Books, New York, 1982.

Imai, M., *KAIZEN – The Key To Japanese Competitive Success,* Random House, New York, 1986.

Kawasaki, G., *Selling the Dream Harper Business*, New York, 1992.

Kiam, V., *Going For It,* Fontana/Collins, Glasgow, 1987.

Kyosaki, R., *If You Want to be Rich and Happy Don't go to School,* Excellerated Learning Publishing, San Diego, 1992.

Maltz, M., *Psycho-Cybernetics,* Melvin Powers, Wilshire Book Company, Hollywood, 1960.

McCormack, M.H., *The 110% Solution*, Pan Books, London, 1990.

McCormack, M.H., *What They Still Don't Teach You at Harvard Business School*, Bantam Books, New York, 1989.

Peters, T., *Thriving on Chaos,* Pan Books, London, 1989.

Peters, T., *Liberation Management,* Pan Books, London, 1993.

Ringer,R.J., *Million Dollar Habits*, Fawcet Crest, New York, 1990.

Sheehy, G., *Pathfinders*, Bantam Books, New York, 1982.

Townsend, R., *Up the Organisation,* Coronet Books, Hodder & Stoughton, London, 1970.

Waitley, D., *Being The Best*, Pocket Books, New York, 1988.

Waterman, R.H., *The Renewal Factor*, Bantam Books, New York, 1988.

References

[1] Tom Peters, *Liberation Management*, Pan Books, London, 1993, pp.532, 533.

[2] Akio Morita, *Made in Japan*, William Collins and Sons, London, 1987, p.226.

[3] R. T. Pascale and A.G. Athos, *The Art of Japanese Management*, Warner Books, New York, 1981.

[4] Mary Granius, *Success Unlimited*, June 1978, p.33-38.

[5] Aristotle, *Nicomachean Ethics, Book 3;11*, Bobbs-Merrill, Indianapolis-New York, 1962, p.81.

[6] Eric Berne, M.D., *Games People Play*, Penguin Books, London, 1967.

[7] Masaaki Imai, *KAIZEN – The Key To Japanese Competitive Success*, Random House, New York, 1986.

[8] Antoine de Saint-Exupery, *The Little Prince*, William Heinemann Ltd, London, 1986.

[9] Referring to a river boat.

[10] Rosabeth Moss Canter, *The Change Masters*, Routledge, London, 1992.

[11] Anwar el-Sadat, *In Search of Identity: An Autobiography*, Harper & Row, New York, 1978.

[12] Frederick Herzberg, quoted in William Dowling, Ed., *Effective Management and the Behavioral Science*, AMACOM, New York, 1982.

[13] Henry Ford with Samuel Crowther, *My Life and Work*, Doubleday & Co., New York, 1922.

[14] Hal Rosenbluth, quoted by Robert McGarvey in "The New Order", *Entrepreneur*, April 1994, p.133.

[15] Maslyn Williams, *Faces of My Neighbour -Three Journeys into East Asia*, William Collins Pty Ltd, Sydney, 1979.

[16] Peter M. Senge, *The Fifth Discipline*, Random House Australia, Sydney, 1992.

[17] Louis Thurstone, *The Nature of Intelligence*, Harcourt Brace Jovanovich, New York, 1924.

[18] Benjamin Hoff, *The Tao of Pooh*, E. P. Dutton, Inc., New York, 1982.

[19] Dan Clark, quoted by Robert McGarvey in *Entrepreneur*, May 1994, p.187.

[20] Akio Morita, *Made in Japan*, William Collins and Sons, London, 1987, p.227.

[21] Warren Bennis, *On Becoming a Leader*, Addison-Wesley Publishing Company, Inc, Reading, MA, 1990.

[22] Albert Bandura, *Social Learning Theory*, Prentice-Hall, Englewood Cliffs, NJ, 1977, p.12.

[23] Dr. An Wang, *Lessons*, Addison-Wesley Publishing Company, Inc, Reading, MA, 1986.

[24] Richard Bach, *Jonathan Livingston Seagull*, Turnstone Press Ltd., London, 1973.

[25] quoted in Sheridan M. Tatsuno, *Created in Japan*, HarperBusiness, London, 1990.

[26] Sheridan M. Tatsuno, *Created in Japan*, HarperBusiness, London, 1990.

[27] T.W. Kang, *Gaishi – The Foreign Company in Japan*, HarperCollins Publishers, New York, 1990.

[28] Joe Girard, quoted by Del Reddy and Eileen Courter in "Let's Make a Deal", *Entrepreneur*, August 1994, p.96.

[29] Gerald Jampolsky, M.D., *One Person Can Make a Difference*, Bantam Books, New York, 1990.

[30] Richard Bach, *Jonathan Livingston Seagull*, Turnstone Press Ltd., London, 1973.

[31] Mortimer Adler, "How to Mark a Book", *Saturday Review of Literature*, July 6, 1940.